VIA Folios 20

ETHNICITY

Joseph Tusiani

ETHNICITY

Selected Poems

Edited with two essays
by
Paolo Giordano

BORDIGHERA PRESS

Library of Congress Control Number: 2012936722

Printed in the United States.

Published by
BORDIGHERA PRESS
John D. Calandra Italian American Institute
25 W. 43rd Street, 17th Floor
New York, NY 10036

VIA Folios 20, reprint
ISBN 978–1–59954–046–7

Table of Contents

To Joseph

Joseph Tusiani

ETHNICITY

Selected Poems

Edited with two essays

by

Paolo Giordano

To Cosma Siani

GENTE MIA

SONG OF THE BICENTENNIAL

I.

What would my life have been
had I remained where I was born? What dreams
would I be dreaming now? I cannot even
compare my human state
with that of a plant plucked
from its salubrious ground
and placed elsewhere under a roof for heaven.
Just as the high decree of Fate to me,
incomprehensible
my every question will forever be
to the eternal unity of all —
mountain and rock that form it,
ocean and waves that make it, clouds and sky,
and sun and light. Sunder all this — you have
erosion, desert, and abyss and night.
Yet I have ceased to be
the man I was; the roots wherefrom I sprung
are somewhere else instead. Deracinated —
is this the word that somewhat hides the grief
of one uprooted and no longer young?

What would my life be now
if I were still with my familiar trees?

II.

Let me tonight be wondering about
the shape of every star —
not the unbounded magma that confounds
my human thinking that at best is doubt

nor the translucent sounds
that from the center of infinities
charge the celestial bodies near and far,
creating suns beyond the sun I know.

The shape — let me be wondering about
the shape of stars that glow,
for something tells me that I too was born
under the sign of one
formed like an ocean liner going far,
crowded with silent men called emigrants —
my ethnic star.

III.

Do I regret my origin by speaking
this language I acquired? Do I renounce,
by talking now in terms of only dreams,
the sogni of my childhood? What has changed
that I had thought unchangeable in me?
Yet something's changed — and what, I do not know.
Now every thought I think, each word I say
detaches me a little more from all
I used to love — your faces, ancient friends,
and all our phrases of so much delight
as needed no translation in my mind.

Mother, I even wonder if I am
the child I was, the little child you knew,
for you did not expect your little son
to grow apart from all that was your world,
the world that he saw first with your own eyes —
simple and untranslatable, composed
of one unclouded clarity of light.
Yet of a sudden he was taught to say
'Mother' for Mamma, and for cielo 'sky'.
That very day, we lost each other. Now
I know you look at me as though I were
a little more and yet a little less
than what a son — your little child — should be.
Oh, they have taught me to translate all things —
even my very self — into some new
and old infinity of roots and boughs,
so that I wonder whether I am old
or whether I am new beneath the sky,
beneath the cielo of my long-lost land.

IV.

My long-lost land was one that,
when snows enveloped it,
did not erase a sun that
still in my dream was lit.

But simple was the dream that
in all my fancy shore —
as simple as a gleam that
speaks of a sunken sun:

papier-mâché instead of
true shepherds, painted moss

for a pre-April meadow,
for living light the gloss

of crayon exercises
in every corner glued:
there, made of many sizes,
my cosmic marvel stood.

'Twas my presepe, full of
tu scendi dalle stelle —
the only song and rule of
intime cose belle.

But now my new-found land is
the western world, this new,
mysterious Atlantis
where men like me and you,

called immigrants, are silent
when Silent Night is sung
on this Manhattan Island
by people old and young,

by all save those, like me
and you, uprooted friend,
who think of Italy —
our lost presepe land.

V.

Two languages, two lands, perhaps two souls?
I dare not ask these flowers I know well,
each of them making its one calyx bright.
Nor can I question that forbidding oak:

though low and long, its roots
cease at the hindrance of the nearest brook
as if abhorring alienness of ground.
Then, who will solve the riddle of my day?
Two languages, two lands, perhaps two souls...
Am I a man or two strange halves of one?
Somber, indifferent light,
setting before me with a sneer of glow,
because there is no answer to my plight
I find some solace only in this thought —
that maybe, just as this revolving earth
must not proclaim your triumph all at once,
I too must be, while waiting for my dawn,
the night of my own self.
Or maybe, just as your unbridled flame
would, undivided, scald this hemisphere
and turn it into ashes, I fulfill
my human fate by giving you, O sun,
a chance of mercy on my helpless life.

VI.

Civis Americanus Sum: I swore
allegiance to the Flag of Fifty Stars:
long live America for ever more!

Now I belong where countless wounds and scars
create a morning and an epic song
that neither time nor silence ever mars.

Now, only now for every suffered wrong
do I discover who I am at last —
the multitudinous Italian throng.

I am the present for I am the past
of those who for their future came to stay,
humble and innocent and yet outcast.

I am the dream of their eternal day —
the dream they dreamed in mines bereft of light —
I am their darkness and their only ray,

their silence and their voice: I speak and write
because they dreamed that I would write and speak
about their unrecorded death and night.

O glory! I'm the bread they came to seek,
the vine they planted to outvanquish doom,
their most majestic and enduring peak.

For this my life their death made ample room.

ETHNICITY

O new awareness of my ancient light,
What's then so new about this earth of mine?
Though everything you seem to redefine,
'Tis but a tale of night excluding night.
So I discover what in me was bright
Long before brightness was allowed to shine,
Able at last to trace and underline
Letter and spirit of my simple right.

Now, only now the truth I understand —
That, born as mortal as a bird or bat,
Man ever longs for some immortal land.
Brother, you came from Erin, I from Rome,
And others started hence — but what of that?
Today migration and tomorrow home.

COLUMBUS DAY IN NEW YORK

Poor Joel Barlow, your Columbiad
unwrote itself for lack of salty spray.
Here is the epic of Columbus Day
reduced to an innocuous parade

where mayoral dreamers grin in competition,
endorsed (or almost) by the Governor,
and politicians who are neither-nor
turn on Italian smiles as cars' ignition.

It does not matter. This is gente mia,
for I can see (is there a lump in his throat?)
dear Christopher Columbus on a float
called for all time to come Santa Maria.

How beautiful he beams! He has the eyes
of my Grandfather, and his calloused hand;
he is the immigrant of every land
unhappy in his happy paradise,

misunderstood in all this understanding
gold of the Indian summer round his brow,
unable to forget the Ocean now
when he should but recall the joy of landing.

Look closer! There's Grandfather, come this year
to represent Columbus on his float.
A hero and the worthiest of note,
he is the very one no crowd will cheer

tomorrow when the town goes back to work;
but look at him today, today at last,
in all the greatness of his humble past —
the new Columbus conquering New York.

He brings the best credentials to be he —
faith in his glance to win the fighting waves,
dream of free people and despair of slaves
to conquer a new land ultimately.

So here he is today, today at last,
riding atop his bright Santa Maria,
the navigator of the gente mia,
light of my future, darkness of his past,

the one who came to dig (for dig we must)
for the high glory of the subway tracks,
the immigrant who died and yet still lacks
identity with this American dust.

ELLIS ISLAND

Why a museum now? No monument
immortalizes gravity of pain
save its occurrence — a mere memory
    fading from year to year
    into a painless name.
Once more the Ocean woos the firmament,
the firmament the Ocean once again:
in this new peace who dares accuse the sea
    of ancient death and fear,
    the sky of endless shame?

How narrow yet how noumenal is still
this famous island! Fervent in the sun,
it is as tranquil as a land should be —
    a place where God may start
    creating worlds anew
or where, forgetful of his own free will,
any new Adam may, for daily fun,
embrace his Eve in perfect harmony.
    How guiltless seems this part
    of America to you!

Yet on this very isle — how long ago? —
man's sobbing deafened every tidal roar
and tears eclipsed the happy-reigning light.
    Thousands had come in hope
    and thousands in despair,
for the first time forgetting every woe,
for the last time remembering every war,

only believing in their human right —
    freedom from king or pope,
    freedom to breathe new air.

O beauty yet O Babel of the world!
What bureaucratic difficulty found
a written cross not good enough to be
    a proper signature?
    Emaciated, pale,
back to their countries laborers were hurled,
who were already on the envied ground
eager to build America the Free —
    the innocent and pure
    forbidden to prevail.

O grief and agony beneath the glance
of Goddess Liberty! What should have been
the first and last oasis of the earth
    became the last and first
    concentration camp,
another jail, another circumstance,
one more disaster and one more chagrin
after the unforeseen disgrace of birth.
    Once hungry and accursed,
    always the tragic tramp!

Who are you, brother, finally allowed
to land now and most legally set foot
on this still virgin Continent you need?
    This Continent needs you,
    but this you must not know.
Only remember that you are the crowd,
the ever-famished and the ever-brute,
the father with a dozen sons to feed,
    the inexpensive crew,
    the expendable foe.

11

It does not matter what you say, what tongue
you speak, what saint or demon you invoke:
you're not America but she is you —
    a bond of force and faith,
    a chain of love and loss.
You'll be tomorrow the surviving throng,
the roots and still the branches of the oak,
the antiquated and therefore the new,
    the life that springs from death,
    the ore that comes from dross.

Why a museum now? Set here, instead,
a roller coaster that from earth to sky,
from sky to earth, may all grandchildren bring
    without reminding them
    of tragedies bygone.
By old injustices are new ones bred:
this is (oh, let me dream) the reason why
our Ellis Island, land of suffering,
    should be the diadem
    of the still winning sun.

THE ITALIAN GOAT

If per contraria we know all things —
    white from black, peace from war —
clear is the reason why these murmurings,
    so indistinct before,

are now the voice from some prenatal place
    of human helplessness
where the despair of my Italian race
    started this restlessness.

But how — how can it be this easy green
    suggests volcanic red;
this friendly river, blood I've never seen
    and yet, I, too, have shed?

Maybe the sap that nurtures all that grows
    springs from uneasy thought,
binding forever new and ancient woes
    with justice that was not

and yet should be, just as this beauty is
    and will most surely be
around these trees when I am chrysalis
    out of this present me.

So I am here yet there, part of this calm
    and part of all that storm —
the center and circumference, the qualms
    and questions of the norm,

the vision and the visionary, man
     and man's own effigy.
Will someone tell me, though, how greenness can
     a red remembrance be?

Apollo here, a nimble gentle hound,
     jumps over a green gate
and plays with Daphne evermore around
     her kittens' easy fate.

But somewhere else (I see it, I am there)
     a poor Italian's goat,
finding its portioned little bush too spare
     and scratchy down its throat,

and therefore hungry like its owner — look! —
     has impudently run
over the fence of Dr. Vandercook,
     awaiting with his gun.

Seeing his helpless sole support sprawled dead
     on the forbidden dew,
Mr. I-talian (is it I, instead?),
     his fist raised in the blue

walks toward the slayer, muttering again,
     "I woulda pay . . ." but he,
being a dago, can as such be slain
     with all impunity.

Another shot of the same faultless gun,
     and goat and goatherd everyone can see
dead in the greenness of the trespassed lawn,
     as guilty as can be.

Great Hudson! For the dead of long ago
    the living have no tears,
but you and this Atlantic Ocean know
    after a hundred years.

Delightful breeze on this wet greenness playing,
    magical murmurings
of leaves so subtly to the summer swaying
    as round a rainbow wings,

blow on till I forget all that is red —
    trauma of blood and fire —
blow on, blow on till I absorb instead
    only this verdant choir.

THE BARREL-ORGAN

with apologies to Alfred Noyes

Music, music, only music is the language of the heart,
so new music I am playing in the heart of old New York.
Father says we have nobody but the music and the stork:
here's a song for everybody, here's a song I know by heart.

> Grandfather long ago
> a piece of land had he,
> but God makes nothing grow
> in southern Italy.

> Grandfather was as strong
> as any southern man,
> and knew that it was wrong
> not to work and work again.

> So in his piece of land
> harder he worked that year,
> sowing with his own hand,
> praying with all his fear.

> But when the new spring came
> with swallows from the sea,
> his land was not the same,
> as Father said to me.

> Grandfather sighed: "At last,
> at last we'll have some bread!"

16

His little land was fast
blossoming green and red.

"What do you know!" said he,
who could not hide his tears,
"God has remembered me
after so many years."

Music, music, only music is the language of the heart,
so new music I am playing in the heart of old New York.
I am late, I overslept, and no child should oversleep.
I'm American by birth, but Five Points is my true land.
Back with this my barrel-organ, that's my torture and my toy,
though I look like other children I'm a poor Italian boy.

Grandfather, most excited,
numbered each stalk of wheat,
and blessed the Sun Almighty
that was so mild and sweet.

The sky smiled blue and deep
as Baby Jesus' eyes.
Grandfather said: "We'll reap
a little paradise."

His land grew large and new,
and rich as altar gold,
the sky more deep and blue,
the sun more bright and bold.

So one day . . .

Music, music, only music is the language of the heart,
so new music I am playing in the heart of old New York.
Father says we have nobody but the music and the stork.

But there's something new today. There is also — come and see —
little Monkey Mary-Ann, that is prettier than me.
She is worth a lot of money and must always be well fed,
so I give her, when she's hungry, half the portion of my bread.
If she dies (O God, forbid), we can't buy another one,
but 'tis nothing if another poor Italian boy is dead.
Music, music, only music is the language of the heart . . .
(Thank you, lady. Mary-Ann thanks you also very much)
So new music I am playing in the heart of old New York:
Father says we have nobody but the music and the stork.

> One day a sudden rumble
> thundered from hill to town:
> a hailstorm came to tumble
> in blinding torrents down.
>
> Sins of the world had so
> offended God anew,
> He ordered winds to blow
> as He alone can do.
>
> Only between God's hand
> and every mortal sin
> there was Grandfather's land,
> caught in between.
>
> In less than a half hour
> a whole year's dream fell dead:
> goodbye, Grandmother's flour,
> goodbye, Grandfather's bread!
>
> Grandfather did not curse,
> though wholly bent and low,
> but he was spared much worse,
> dying before the snow.

Before he died, Grandfather
had but one thing to say.
"This is no land," he said to Father;
"I curse you if you stay."

Music, music, only music...

I, Costantino Brumidi

I, Costantino Brumidi, declare
that Art and Liberty go hand in hand.
Pardon me, gentlemen, I did not know
that I had company. At times, you see,
I interrupt my work and, to be able
to study with detachment the effect
of this or that detail — that is, to weigh
upon my very eyelids light and shade —
I talk out loud, uttering sentences
I would not dare direct but at myself.
'Tis an old habit that, one day, in Rome
nearly destroyed me. Brush in hand, I stood
up on the scaffolding sixty feet high
and, unaware of the whole world below,
was all intent on studying a dot
of heavy white placed in the very midst
of a blue iris, calculating distance
and therefore dimness whereby to determine
its fullest sheen and faintest radiance.
I would have wished at the same time to be
up where I was and down where I was not —
a privilege God grants to but a few
of His innumerable Saints — and so,
maybe to tease myself or God above,
out loud I said (and you are free to think
of what the echo added to my words:)
"Your Holiness, where are you? Why so low?
Should I then say Your Lowliness?" "Right here,"

he answered, "We are here to see you work
and not to hear you talk." I almost fell.
'Tis an old habit I cannot discard.
But, gentlemen, what was I saying? Oh,
that Art and Liberty go hand in hand?
I meant much more than that — the two are one
just as a living plant is its own sap.
Therefore you will allow me to refute
all that you say against me — that a man
born in an alien land and loyal only
to laws and principles of foreign art
will fail to capture the most basic traits
of painting that you call American.
American? But say: Does a new place
dictate new confines to the free-born soul?
Or is it false the soul's the only law
an artist has to heed? Then neither school
nor region can avail. Here I am painting,
oh, yes, according as I have been taught
by masters such as Michelangelo
and Raphael and Titian, but to me
my tool is not my art — my freedom is.
And could I ever in a better land
have found such freedom as I have in yours?
Your land! This land! But mine has yet to see
its greatest glory. The beloved shores
are not yet free, and the all-mantling light
of the free sun envelops their expanse
as if in golden irony of day.
Yes, art is pure and free, but if your eye
sees only blood and sacrifice of youth,
how will you reconcile within yourself
freedom of vision and denial of life?
Your very brush reminds you of the gun
a despot wields: so you begin to wonder

why, of all people, you are there, up there,
high on a scaffolding that saves your skin,
while others bravely fight down in the streets,
painting with real blood their masterpiece —
the final triumph of the fatherland.

Too old for action on the battlefield
but not too old for dreams of freedom, here
in this beloved land at last I am,
eager to prove that . . . Gentlemen, where are you?
Have I perhaps offended you?. . . Well then,
back to my work. There is no other way:
this Nike must be given shield and sword
to blunt and break the daring of the foe.
Yes, but her sword must have as bright a blade
as Cincinnatus' plough, for, now I know,
no difference exists between the two:
one cannot be without the other's life.
So back to work now. Washington, dear father,
it is not difficult to limn your features,
for men like you forever paint themselves
so that we simply copy what they did.
But why am I so dizzy?. . . God! . . . My God!. . .
Somebody help me! . . . Help! . . .

THE DAY AFTER THE FEAST

Our Lady of Mount Carmel in the Bronx,
back in your niche you seem to be quite pleased,
    as all your children are,
whether or not they wear your Scapular.

Last night your children were the chanting throngs
behind your statue and the parish priest,
    and now they once again
are what they were — unknown, hard-working men.

Yes, you are pleased remembering this new
Procession in your honor, with a glare
    of altar boys in red,
a band, balloons slow-floating overhead,

and from the sidewalks people throwing you
signs-of-the-cross and kisses and a prayer:
    three hours of paradise
quite visible in all our mortal eyes.

This morning everybody's back to work
as if no holiday had ever been,
    yet everybody's more
resigned to life than ever, ever before.

Now stands are being felled, and old New York
is all the more the town where some begin
    what others will complete,
the city where we hardly know our street.

Roaring impassive and iconoclastic,
two Sanitation trucks devour and crush
    under metallic teeth
the most impressive artificial wreath

along with cardboard boxes, empty plastic
bottles, confetti, in a raucous rush
    that nothing spares — not even
the remnants of man's festive dream of heaven.

And so on our 187th Street
and Arthur Avenue life once again,
    vociferous and bold,
revolves around a marketplace of old

where, bargaining for codfish or for meat,
old women reminisce of where and when
    codfish and meat were two
of all the luxuries they never knew,

and in the meantime, touching here and there,
they taste an olive and a crumb of cheese
    they do not mean to buy
("it's not so good," which means it's much too high).

O Holy Mother, bless our market square!
This is my Little Italy, and these
    are still (you know I'm right)
the very ones who honored you last night,

the very ones who, knowing earthly woe
and need for solace, love and loss on earth,
    here in this neighborhood
astir with cries of necessary food,

were wise enough to build (how long ago?)
a church near-by for wedding, birth, and death —
    the easy sky they share
close to yet far from every daily care —

your church, O Blessed Mother, where I, too,
just looking at your lovely face, forget
    the tragedy of one
for want of bread uprooted from his sun,

one of the countless immigrants that you,
year after year, see kneeling at your feet,
    still asking to be blest
with food on earth and faith in heaven's rest.

LETTER TO SAN GENNARO

Dear San Gennaro, if in Paradise,
as I am sure, no weed of envy grows,
you must be clapping your ethereal hands
as I my mortal ones, now that — look there! —
Saint Anthony is being borne aloft,
this pallid Portuguese who left his land
and, with his infant Jesus in his arms
and a perennial lily in his hand,
conquered us so completely that he can,
after so many centuries, still pass
for one of us, and who has even come
with Christopher Columbus to this shore,
waiting for us poor immigrants to found
our Little Italy and little dreams.

There he is passing, blissful in the freshness
of his Franciscan wool, from street to street,
reminding every one he's part of us,
one who, in other words, like all of us
began somewhere and ended somewhere else.
This is the reason why we love him so,
although we never met him. And there is,
dear San Gennaro, something else we should
be pardoned for in loving him so much:
because he was an immigrant, he saw
the thirteen things we shall forever need
each single day of this our earthly life.
Your miracle is mighty: twice a year
your blood, as if revived by rain or breeze,

bubbles vermillion like a timeless rose —
the symbol of our lost Vesuvius' glow —
a most enchanting sight that can transform
coagulated darkness into dawn.
But, of his thirteen miracles a day,
most had to do with bread and butter — things
we need, O holy Bishop, more and more.

So there he goes, the owner and the omen
of all the Little Italies on earth,
blessing and blest, adoring and adored.
Children, brown-cowled as little Anthonys,
before the statue in a double row
advance as solemn as sweet imps can be,
most unaware of representing, each
and all of them, their parents' grateful vows.
Behind the Saint, whose plaited tunic glows
with dollar bills that make our pastor gloat
(may his parochial school be paid for soon),
a chanting like a most unruly tide
heaves high and low while clarinets and drums
easily vie with every parish bell.
Onions and peppers, sausages around,
and roller coasters frantic in the air...
O San Gennaro, if the blessed nostrils
of all you Saints are tempted by this earth,
and if the Cherubs of the firmament
envy man's children as I think they do,
I beg you not to tell our Lord on us
or He will think us wealthy for all time.
Saint Anthony will tell you what we are —
still poor, still much in need of daily bread,
still immigrants. But once a year (well, twice:
do not forget September's on its way,
and wait and see what is in store for you)

we like to dream of what we would have been
had we been born in wealth, had we remained
in the fair land where wealth is of the few.
So we are dreaming, immigrants no more,
of being God's true children growing up
in God's true land — not Fate's eternal pawn.
There, we are there: so let us dream some more,
dear San Gennaro, until late tonight.

Tonight, when our Saint Anthony returns,
happily weary from his feast, to sleep
in the Italian section of the sky,
he too will dream of what he saw on earth.
He'll whisper all about it in your ear
tomorrow morning when you stand on line
to pay new homage to the King of kings.
Not far behind you, all the Irish Saints,
visibly hurt and envious, will say,
"Hush! Hush!" But, quite amused upon His throne,
God, I am sure, will understand and smile.

The Ballad of the Coliseum

Once in a village across the Ocean
    to the old fortuneteller went he,
eager to know how rich his future
    in rich America would be.
And the old gypsy, gray and wrinkled,
    read in a big book, wrinkled and gray,
then to the strong young man before her
    these very words she turned to say:

"No earthly monarch will inhabit
    so new a castle as you will
and no man's hand will ever reach you
    beneath your most majestic hill."
Beaming, he begged her, "Of my fortune
    other details, oh, let me learn."
But the old gypsy kept on staring,
    all of a sudden taciturn.

To his well-wishing friends he promised
    he would remember all of them,
but swore to one that he would send her
    the most bejeweled diadem:
for the old gypsy had predicted
    (and the good news had traveled since)
that he'd be rich and even richer
    than any king or royal prince.

"Mother," he said, as he embraced her,
    kissing her dearly one time more,

"Mother, of one thing I am certain —
    that I will let you scrub no floor."
The frail washwoman kissed and kissed him,
    brave to pretend she wasn't sad,
but, oh, her breaking heart was heavy,
    losing the only wealth she had.

The sea, one undulating crystal,
    grew every day more dazzling-white:
maybe the sun was much more lustrous
    or someone's dream had grown more bright.
America at last! O country
    where every street was paved with gold!
Manhattan Island in the sunrise
    the fairest vision to behold!

Vertical petals of a flower
    the tall skyscrapers seemed to stand,
while, countless golden bees about it,
    swarmed all the boats of the new land.
Even more beautiful than Naples,
    New York was there — there was New York.
Angelo's dreams had also landed:
    "When do I start to work — to work?"

To work he started the next morning
    with an Italian laboring throng.
All of them looked so wan, so weary
    to him, so rosy-cheeked and strong.
When that first day of work was ended
    and he lay sleepless on his bed,
he missed his mother, missed his village,
    missed his childhood that was fled.

Another day and still another,
    and then the first and second year . . .

Time passed and then (O God!) a letter
    in a black envelope came here.
"Dear Angelo," it said, "Your mother
    died of a sudden heart attack.
She did not suffer, but kept asking
    until the end, "Has he come back?""

But how could he? With all his savings
    (oh, how he counted them and sighed!)
he bought a blessed one-way ticket
    for one who soon became his bride.
She seemed so frightened at the harbor
    until she saw and smiled at him.
Her tears of joy were much more shining
    than any regal diadem.

All paesani came that evening
    and all together danced and sang,
and one of them who knew the language
    (a little bit of New York slang)
toasted the lovely couple, holding
    a glass of homemade wine aloft:
"I wisha you much 'appinessa
    wit' much amore strong an' soft."

"My friend," another spoke, "a gypsy
    has said that Angelo will die
(a hundred years from now) as wealthy
    as any king beneath the sky."
And everybody laughed. Their laughter
    rippled with warmth the chilly air,
but at that moment up in heaven
    the angels heard a mother's prayer.

Never to miss a work-day, never
    to be in need or, worse, in debt —

Angelo's dream did not envision
    a greater happiness than that.
And so he worked, and lime and mortar
    were his most precious ornaments,
and when he found more work, he treasured
    with greater joy his few more cents.

Many more years went by, and seven
    boys and a girl, American born,
calling him Papa! Papa!, made him
    feel like a king upon a throne.
But to feed eight more mouths our Sire
    from his high throne had to come down
and go wherever a new building
    was being built — uptown, downtown.

Stone and concrete and brick and plaster
    to him were more than trade and tool:
they were a miracle from heaven
    that sent his children all to school.
"Papa," one day his Pietro told him,
    "My teacher said that here at home
we soon will have a Coliseum
    as big and tall as that in Rome:

but what's a Coliseum, Papa?"
    The right reply he could not give,
but said, "It's like a . . . big palazzo
    where kings or presidents must live.
And, by the way, you tell your teacher
    (with great respect do always speak)
that the construction of this building
    begins, I know, this coming week."

Where Central Park in whiteness opens —
    the marble Battleship of Maine —

32

across the street construction started
    amid the smiles of sun and rain.
The deafening din of ten bulldozers
    seemed to create a festive sound:
wheelbarrows, cranes, and sand and trowels
    eagerly waited all around.

There before long the Coliseum
    would rise as magic as its name.
Simply to be one of its builders
    meant — and why not? — to share its fame.
And so our builder every evening,
    sitting at table with his wife —
while all enrapt his children listened —
    counted the blessings of his life.

For, after all, he now was working
    not at an ordinary home,
but a palazzo that was almost
    as big and tall as that in Rome.
To Rome, of course, he'd never traveled
    from his poor southern Italy
but all his children never doubted
    what Papa said so solemnly.

And to his wife he whispered, "Anna,
    this job will last two years or longer.
The pay is good and — let me tell you —
    despite my age I feel much stronger,
well, strong enough to put through college
    (for time's-a-flying) our first son.
He'll be a lawyer — no, a doctor."
    And she replied, "God's will be done."

God's will was done six short months later.
    Angelo said to her, "You know?

I dreamed of Mother. She looked happy,
 and had a special radiant glow.
She told me that our son will make it,
 and be a doctor, if you please.
Just think of it: he'll cure his Papa —
 and Mama too — of all disease."

That day, he left as if in glory —
 the father of a famous man.
The Coliseum in the sunshine
 boasted its half-completed span —
a lofty labyrinth of ramparts,
 a mass of steel and wet cement
that by no blowing wind or thunder
 could broken be or even bent.

Then, if no blowing wind or thunder
 could shake or shatter it at all,
what sudden wrath of hell or heaven
 struck on a hardly finished wall,
bringing it down but in a twinkle
 with the explosion and the roar
as of an avalanche of snow
 or billows breaking on a shore?

Blinding smoke followed, with its darkness
 instantly blotting out the sun,
and dust and dust in rings of doomsday
 almost concealed the damage done.
But spikes and spires in one tangle
 of twisted steel at once appeared,
and, minutes later, sirens sounded,
 louder and louder, wild and weird.

How many dead? How many injured?
 Only one dead — our Angelo.

They looked all over for his body,
    but there was wet cement below
and many a ton of brick above it.
    The futile search was stopped at night,
and by that time the sky was limpid
    and in Manhattan life was bright.

Superbly stands the Coliseum,
    lively with shows in every room.
But say a prayer, all who enter,
    treading on an Italian's tomb —
the most majestic tomb a monarch
    may wish for, whether young or old,
the grave that in a distant village
    a gray, old gypsy had foretold.

THE BALLAD OF FATHER KELLY

Of all the Italian missionaries who came to America, the Dominican Samuel Mazzuchelli (1806-1864) is the most versatile and colorful. He was immigrant-pioneer, priest-healer, architect-builder, financier-administrator, linguist-philologist. The Irish settlers called him "Father Kelly," and the Indians whose language he spoke and made known to scholars worshiped him. He built more than twenty churches and schools, and designed the old Iowa State capitol. But "Father Kelly" remained essentially a priest. He died of pneumonia, which he contracted while on a sick call to one of his Indian parishioners during a blizzard. This Ballad is based on this least-known detail of his life.

"Father, wake up! Wake up! One of your men is dying,
and for your priestly word he more and more is sighing.
Come, Father Kelly, come, for bitterly he's crying:
without the Sacraments the poor old man is dying."

"Then pray for me, my son, that I may not be failing
to bring the Eucharist to one so gravely ailing.
Thickly the snow is falling, strongly the wind is wailing,
but God Himself will go, borne by his servant Kelly."

"Look, Father Kelly," boasts the snow but with no malice,
"what I have done with all these mountains and these valleys.
You are the architect of many a church and palace,
but never have you built so fine and white a chalice."

"Say, Father Kelly," asks the wind more fiercely freezing,
"don't you remember me? Together many a season
we spent on lake and land, but now you're sorely wheezing:
this time you'll die, old man. Oh, I am simply teasing."

"Dear Father Kelly, welcome back to Winnebago,"
the whole wide forest says with a white muffled echo;
"You are so wan and weary: where is your younger Ego?
But welcome to Sioux, welcome to Winnebago!"

"Why are you walking so — so silent?," adds a raven,
half frozen in the whiteness of neither earth nor heaven.
So many Indian tongues you speak, and cannot even,
poor Father Kelly, crow like a Chippewa raven."

"Jesus, my Lord and God, of lasting life true Giver,"
the Father prays, knee-deep in snow, aflame with fever,
"show me the way across this never-ending river
or I'll be late to reach your most devout believer."

"O Father Kelly, listen! This is your master speaking,"
answers the Host on his chest, so heavily breathing and breaking,
"far, far away is still the cottage you are seeking,
but I'm with you: so why are you so sorely shaking?"

"You, O my Lord, I'm bearing Who are True Life forever,"
says Father Kelly, rising with all his burning fever,
"and yet I feel that death has come my days to sever.
I need, my Lord and God, my faith now more than ever."

"If I'm True Life forever, then let's of life be singing,"
replies the Sacred Host that Father Kelly's bringing.
"You fed the famished, healed the sick, and, to me clinging,
made many others share in all your joyous singing.

"Now tell me, Father Kelly: what is it you desire
for all that you have done for me, your Lord and Sire?
Because your love was high, I'll make your merit higher:
so tell me what it is, my son, that you desire."

The frozen forest and the raven prompt together,
"Ask, Father Kelly, ask at once for springtime weather:
tell Him that wind and snow should bow to their Creator
and let the entire earth renew its bud and feather."

"Jesus, my only love," says Father Kelly, trying,
trying in vain to check his truly joyous crying,
"I wish that I could be one of your angels flying
to bring You one more time to the sick and the dying."

"You will, you will," replies the Maker of earth and heaven;
"this and much more, my son, will you be granted and given.
Today you're taking me to one who needs my leaven,
but I myself tomorrow will take your soul to heaven."

Jesus and Father Kelly in the first morning splendor
closer together walk in the snow, bright and tender.
To the warm sun the cold winds of the night surrender,
and finally into the cottage Father and Jesus enter.

The Difficult Word

1.

Father, the tearful bride you left behind
became my mother, for your healthy seed
grew in the loving beauty of her youth
until it blossomed — an anachronistic
spring lighting up a January dawn.
A letter to America was sent
to let you know your baby boy was born.
How you received the long-awaited news
you never told me — whether with your friends
you broke the Prohibition, drinking one
or two forbidden bottles to my health,
or whether, worried by uncertain days,
you only thought of one more mouth to feed.
Let me believe the burden of my birth
brought you at least some respite of delight
or I would wish that babe, so far away,
had been allowed to wish his day undone.

2.

From my first sillabario I learned
the two most awesome letters — P and A:
so with red crayon, at the age of three,
Papà I wrote — an exercise of love
printed beneath my mother's praise of me.
Or was it my first exercise of faith?
I did not even know what father meant,
save that he was a photo on a wall,

the picture of a man whose piercing eyes
(so I was being told) relived in mine.
That letter reached you before Christmas Day,
but I still wonder what it meant to you —
whether, that is, it was a simple word
that with no effort any child would write
or whether from some dim recesses of
human despair it spelled a double grief:
"No husband and no father." Christmas Day
brought me, instead, the mystery of snow —
an omnipresent coldness in the air
with the heart-warming chirping, now and then,
of a bird feeding fledglings in their nest.

3.

When verses became easier than bread
poems I sent you, both to make you proud
of your grown son who did not know you yet
and to illude myself, through warmth of rhymes,
that you had never left, and lack of food
had not been strong enough to separate
husband from wife, father from son. And so
I could relive my childhood in a dream:
flowers I picked on new-born Mays with you;
beaming, I showed my report card to you,
and it was you who took me, hand in hand,
to see the Circus that had come to town,
and then regaled me with a blue balloon
which I, the owner of both sky and sea,
for days and days among my peers displayed
as a bright emblem of my happiness.

4.

Then came the morning when, a child no more —
a man already saddened by the death

of his own country left aflame behind —
I saw you from a ship, saw you alone
(fiction and fact: O blood thicker than water!)
out of the hundreds waiting at the pier.
I had been longing for that hour of hours,
counting my heartbeats, measuring the waves
of the Atlantic Ocean, blue before me.
"Faster," I had been praying, "faster, faster,
ship of my fate!" That picture on the wall
was taking on a shape unknown to me —
a man, a mortal man I did not know
was drawing closer with my very name,
my very face: a man, a dream no more,
a man, the man, my father. It was hard
to reconcile those seven simple days
that sundered all my being from its source
with twenty-three hard years of loneliness.
Yet "Not so fast, oh, not so fast!" a sad
and dismal thought was warning. I can even
recall the two distractions of my mind:
"Columbus was right here. Cabrini, too,
perhaps felt lonely on this very spot."
Oh, but they had no father still to meet.
"Faster, go faster, vessel of my life!"
And so, that morning, of all human things
(fiction and fact: O blood thicker than water!)
I saw you first — but did you first see me?

5.

"That man's my father," more than once I said,
as a command, to every pounding vein,
wishing I could rely on something more
than an old photograph hung on a wall.
But there you were — an ordinary man
who never, hand in hand, had taken me

to see the Circus that had come to town,
a man like all the others in the crowd
joyously waving hands and handkerchiefs,
a stranger looking, so it seemed, at me.
Beside me, lost in her own loneliness,
Mother was smiling at that man, her spouse,
with an enchanting sadness in her eyes,
as if to ask forgiveness for the grief
of twenty-three years showing on her brow
or maybe she herself forgiving fate
for all her youth extinguished silently
in a small mountain village far away.
Far . . . far away . . . Yet, Father, you were near,
and now between us there was only one
obstacle left — a passport to be stamped
and two valises waiting to be checked.
But why was I so suddenly afraid,
with all my thoughts receding far away?
Papà! I spoke this word when kissing you,
but it was not my heart — it was my mind
that prompted it, this most difficult word.
The word that I knew best and practiced most,
the very first and most familiar word
became the hardest to pronounce: Papà!
I heard its hollow ring within my soul
and felt the anguish of its emptiness.

6.

Oh, we have grown apart — you with no son,
I with no father. Emigration's last
and most uncharted tragedy is this —
slowly it forces people to adjust
to want of love, anticipating death.
A reunited family means only
reunion of faces, not of feelings.

42

Or I would not with so much envy think
of flocks of birds migrating to new climes
yet still together in the hostile wind.
Father, when spring is miracle again,
the same birds fly to their remembered nest;
but, Father, you and I cannot return
to what did not exist. So call me still
by my first name if still your lips are slow
to say the word you shculd have always said
till it became a meaning in your soul.
Let us (if faith begets but suffering)
forgive each other in the name of love:
even unnamed, a flame is warm and bright.

ODE TO AN ILLITERATE POET

Grandmother spoke in parables: she was
one you would call illiterate. To tell me
to come home early, before dark, she would
remind me that the hen, worth less than man,
goes to the coop before the shadows come,
or she would warn (was she the mountain's mind?)
that one who walks with night has death as friend.
They had not taught her how to read or write
for those were years when poverty was school.
The only thing she wrote with her own hand
was when a sullen man in uniform
guided her fingers on a piece of paper
and made her sign a cross — a cross whereby
she was acknowledging receipt of all
that of her son was left — a handkerchief,
a letter not yet sent, a rosary,
and a small picture of her, stained with blood.
It was Grandmother shaped my day and night,
for she knew not the syntax of the few.
I never ate a precious slice of stale bread
without her telling me Christ too was poor.
I never drank a drop of cool well water
without her teaching me God made the rain.
And if I still was thirsty, she would say
there is no water on the battlefield.
I'd not yet seen a shepherd or a sheep
and yet I knew them both, for, when the thunder
suddenly spoke of anger in the sky,
I always heard this prayer from her lips,

"Run, little orphan shepherd, run, little sheep:
the coldest cave can be a mother's arms."
She was so sad and wise, I wonder now
what really made her soul so wise and sad.
For there is nothing that I hear or do
that does not link me with some ancient loss
or make me part of anguish not my own.
I was fourteen when Grandma died; but now,
at forty, I know well she is not dead.

IN MEMORIAM: JOE PISANO

Uncle, I know now why this spring began
so strangely cold: it wanted to prepare me
for this new coldness round my life. Today
is the day after, the beginning of
your wake, our wake, my slow becoming used
to thinking you as cold as snow, as silent
as unremembered Mays. In a few hours
you will be lying in your timeless bier,
who never in your life at any time
could understand an idle afternoon,
and I — I must acknowledge with no tears
the end of part of me by seeing you
hopelessly dead among still living blooms.
Now even insignificant details
are worth a lifetime, for I must recall
what suit you wear for your last social feast,
and if your features, set eternally,
form a last smile or a first frantic fear.
In a short while I'll see you as you are,
who well remember, Uncle, as you were —
the only man who brought me early figs
that (is it true?) bore witness to your faith
in nature's still maternal amplitude.
"Figs from my backyard!" you announced to me
whenever, unannounced yet welcome most,
you wished to tell me of Italian skies
here in the midst of this Atlantic fog.
Or was it simply that you only needed
the least excuse to justify yourself?
Now that you're gone into undying sunshine
why is the small tree that was all your pride

suddenly dead? It only took three weeks
to end three quarters of a century.
This you already know; but do you also
know that, deprived of your attentive touch,
your only fig tree wished no more to live?
It followed your example: it became
as pale as you, as withered and as dry
there in the backyard that is yours no more.
How will you justify your life to me
now that the simplest of your dreams has ceased
together with your breath? How shall I still,
after all this, believe that of man's deeds
the purest and most innocent endures?
Or is your dream at last becoming true
in this my very questioning, in these
last remnants of your long-uprooted life?
Uncle, dear Uncle, how afraid I am
of facing you, in a few hours, tonight.
Not that I dread the sight of absent life,
who often have desired it in myself.
Only I do not promise I'll recall,
in the right order, all the things I should
for the last time and maybe for the first:
a laborer's hands so strong and gnarled and now
so unaccustomed to the rosary beads,
an immigrant's large forehead that contained
until last night the basic truths of life,
and maybe still that smile, that sad half-smile
that gave and begged forgiveness of the world.

O Mother's only brother,
I am afraid to face your features, calm
in their irrevocable lifelessness —
the features that will tell me (O my God!)
of one more death and one more funeral.

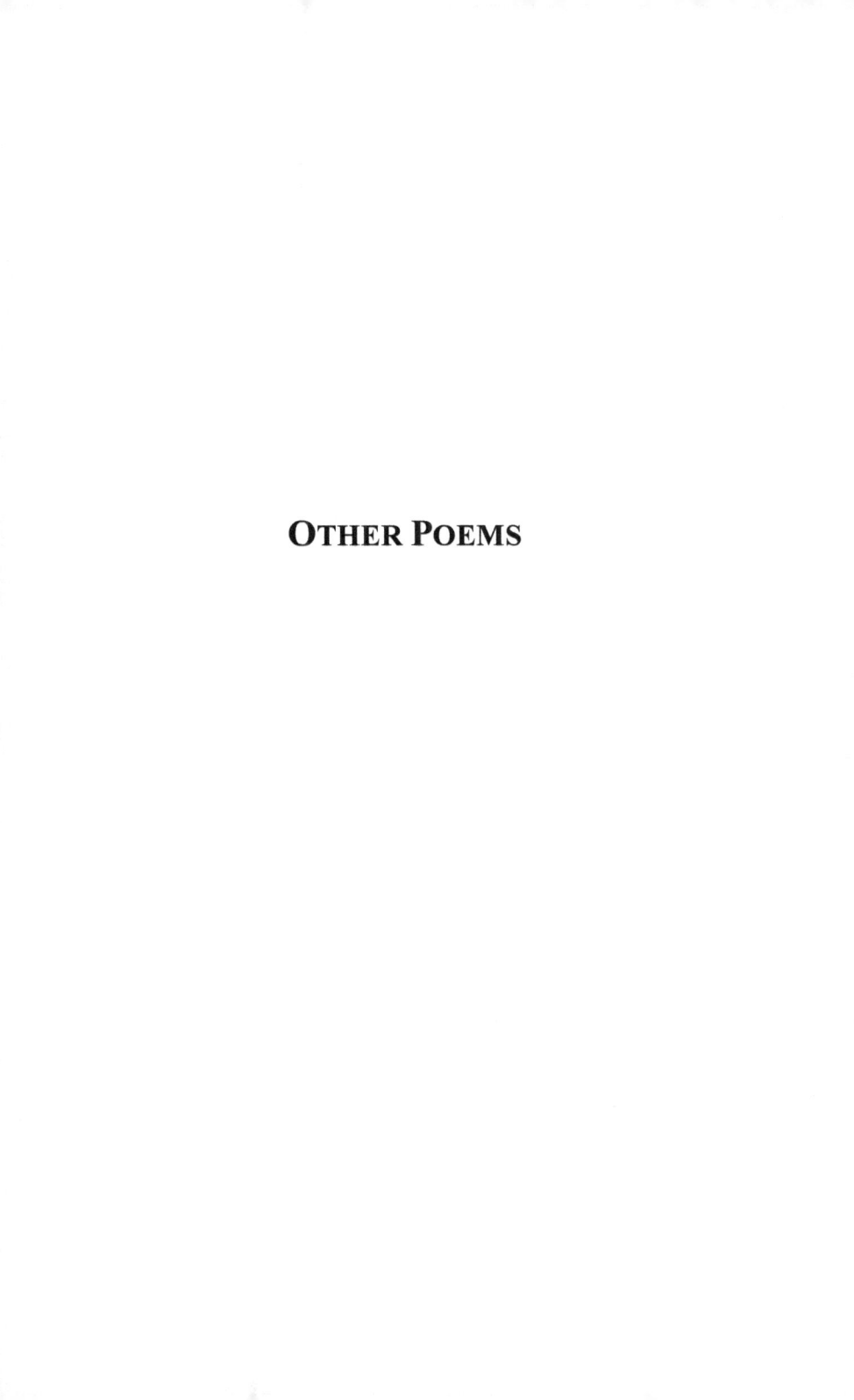

OTHER POEMS

TO MY FATHER (THE DAY AFTER HIS FUNERAL)

I have to make an urgent call to Heaven:
    is faith the area code?
I have to tell the man who was my Father
    what he already knows
and I can understand only today.
    I want to thank him for
fixing, his last few days upon this earth,
    so many little things
for his impractical son — a lamp, a clock,
    a radio, a chair,
and at the very end a sliding door.
    Is faith the area code?
For I must call him now, before he enters
    the higher, deeper spheres
of his eternity where human words
    can be perceived no more.
This I must tell him — that I know at last
    the only reason why
all of a sudden he grew restless, almost
    frantic because of love:
sensing he had to go, he wished to leave
    each little thing in order
so as to spare his son the alien task
    of coming down to earth.
For well the man who was my Father knew
    that simple things that have
nothing to do with the much simpler life
    of either grass or light
frighten my whole existence day by day

and make me call for help.
The only reason? Oh, he tried to be,
    with the most simple pretext
of fixing here a lamp and there a clock,
    a radio, a chair,
closer to me than he had ever been
    all of his life before.
But I must tell him that I understand,
    and thank him for his love.
So will somebody tell me, for God's sake,
    how I can reach at once
the man who was my Father? He must know
    before it is too late,
before he is too dazzled by God's light
    to see or still remember
that he has left a grieving son behind —
    a son so deep in night.

ETHNIC QUARTET

I. NONNO GIUSEPPE

Should a small burgeon question its own tree?
Yet I was only seven years of age
when, proud of my grandfather who had built
skyscrapers in America as tall
as seven hundred giants all in one,
I wondered why a hero such as he
could not have learned the day of his own birth.
"Nonno, when were you born?" and he would say,
fondling his big moustache as if to find
a way to make me understand a truth
too regal for my mind to penetrate,
"The year our King Emmanuel was born."
But, unaware of courts and purple cloaks,
I wanted to know more — the day and month
of his appearance on our common earth.
"But, Nonno," I insisted, "tell me when."
Once again stroking his moustache with pride,
he would reply to me, "See, I was born
together with the Virgin Mary." What?
"But how can this be, Nonno? You are old,
but not so old as Jesus's mother is,
who lived so many centuries ago."
At this, Grandfather with a childish glee,
as if desirous to confound the clerks
of City Hall and City Hall itself,
said, "I, unlike your dad and you, was born
during the great Novena of the great
Immaculate Conception." In his words

the revelation of the great event
sounded so truly great it made the birth
of other people just a worthless day.
I felt so cheated in that radiance
I hated those who made my birth a date
and not the mystery a birth should be.

II. Nonna Carolina

Come, Nonna Carolina, come, you too,
to this reunion of roots tonight.
You burned the longest candle on this earth,
which simply means you knew how to protect
your little flame against the blowing wind
or maybe that no cruel wind at all
for some odd reasons ever came your way.
At ninety-six you wanted still to live,
and rightly so; they had not asked you yet
which boy or girl (check first the family!)
deserved your grandson's or granddaughter's hand.
Therefore you wondered, when the priest appeared
to give you last Communion (not yet!),
how a thin wafer could replace true bread.
So you recovered, and were shocked to hear
that, without asking your permission first,
they had already paid someone to sew
the dress you were to wear on your last day.
You tried it on and found it much too short
(what would Nonno Giuseppe think of you
after so many years of widowhood?).
When alterations were completed (two
more inches, please!), you liked the thing you saw.
"Now put it carefully away," you said,
"and when I need it I will let you know."

Meanwhile far more important, urgent things
were there for you to see and comment on —
your great-granddaughter's lipstick (wash it off!),
your great-grandson's first secret cigarette
(what did he try to do, burn down the house?),
and who was talking in the street and why —
solemn events you witnessed from your chair
for one more year. And then the day arrived
when, feeling suddenly so warm and cold,
with your own eyes you wanted to make sure
your special dress had not one wrinkle on it
(what would Nonno Giuseppe think of you —
that you had turned into a sloppy wife?).
You looked so lovely in your lovely dress
I'm sure Nonno Giuseppe once again,
that very evening, fell in love with you.

III. Nonno Michelarcangelo

You, second Grandpa that I never knew,
maybe you are the one I should know best.
Dead when your daughter was just one day old,
you do not know I have, because of you,
all of these years mistaken until now
meaning of birth for mystery of death.
I have been told that, as you lifeless lay
next to the cradle of that baby girl
who was to be the source of this my day,
over that cradle a black ribbon hung
as the sole emblem of both love and loss.
Somebody even spoke (the mountain's rules
were merciless) of choking that first stir
which in its smallness mimicked your last breath,
therefore insulting your enormous end.

There, Grandpa, I was there, in that one room
where women did not know whether to mourn
a sturdy man pneumonia had killed
or to rejoice in life, which once again,
despite your final immobility,
reminded them that loss and love are one.
Out of that sorrow this my heart began,
beating the days that bring me back to you,
Grandfather, whom my mother never knew
and I for this one reason know quite well,
so very well I now can even guess
why we so loved each other instantly,
who did not even meet beneath this sun.

IV. NONNA LUCIA

Nonna Lucia, is it really true
you scrubbed the floors of Don Saverio's home,
and washed his priestly cassocks and his shirts
and all his sisters' and his nieces' gowns
because you could not pay for the one truth
you needed most — your *Buon Passaggio* Mass?
Your *Buon Passaggio*! If you did not *pass*
from earth to heaven in the grace of God,
who ever will? Not I, who, were I Christ,
would have but told you from the depth of life,
"Woman, thy faith has saved thee: go in peace!,"
but, being only man, would now consign
good Don Saverio to hell and worse.
Nonna, forgive me. . . . Too much aching love
has made me blasphemous. I will therefore
only remember I should praise the Lord
for the great joy that made you always shun
the operation that would have restored

your failing sight so that your savings (almost
eight hundred lire, all your lifetime's sweat)
could buy me suits and shoes and books to read.
Then lead me, blind Grandmother (here's my hand),
into the world of your eternal light
where Jesus preaches His beatitudes
and, no more weeping, people such as you
around Him reign — bright rubies on His ring.

DIALOGUE

Nonno Giuseppe, ninety years ago,
had not one thing in common with a man
called Bishop Scalabrini. Distant towns
such as Piacenza he had never seen,
and great cathedrals maybe meant to him
a farm to buy, much larger than his dream.
And yet Grandfather and the Bishop met
as pit and pulpit finally were one.
They recognized each other instantly
and, though one spoke in Latin and the other
replied in his Gargano dialect,
the two felt like twin brothers home at last.
But what could they have possibly discussed —
the man with pick and shovel and no shirt
and the high prelate with the pastoral?
Oh, on much sorrow they exchanged their views,
such as the Crucifixion of God's Son —
something a laborer already knew.
One day, back to the earth and to the sun
out of the night of his Altoona mine,
forgetful of his soot and all his dirt,
Grandfather tried to kiss the Bishop's ring
as he had done on Confirmation Day;
instead, the Bishop grabbed the old man's hand,
and kissed it, saying, "Christ I kiss in you".

FATHER CHINO

Discoverer of the Peninsular Shape of Lower California

Where are you going, Father Chino, late,
so late in this our Californian night?
The sky's awash with whiteness of the moon,
which, blending with the splashing of the sea,
reminds you of the distant snows of Trent.
Where are you going, Father Chino? Spent
into the chasm of companion lights
is the forbidding comet that you saw
ablaze over the globe of frightened men,
who're maybe still now watching in their dreams
the perilous enchantment of its tail.
Are you pursuing other unknown stars
maybe to spot God's lofty dwelling place
and see what rooms He has reserved for you?
Go home and rest! Though built of mud and straw,
a hut on terra firma shelters us
from enmity of heaven and of hell
such as is brewing in these churning waves.
Or are you courting death, death to avoid?
Go back, before, forgetful of the Cross
that you have tied as mast on your canoe,
the ocean roars its triumph over God.
Invincible? But, Father, you're a man
and, being such, cannot outvanquish fate.

What are you doing? In the sudden crash
of this new thunderstorm where will you go?
No Indians can hear or save you now;

the leaden voice of Nature conquers all . . .
'Tis useless talking to a mountaineer
who, even in the middle of despair,
thinks that the billows of the sea are rocks
wherefrom to call his victory on earth.
Maybe he is a fool and maybe not —
for, while the elements pretend to be
as fierce as God is not, he still believes
that the one Goodness that created man
will not, by killing him, itself destroy.
So there he is, cartographer and priest,
tracing upon a map the wonders of
the Trinity's complexities revealed
in Unity of curves and cliffs and gulfs —
the lower California assessed
as one more marvel of God's loveliness.
Maybe he is a fool and maybe not,
for — tell me this — who cares whether a land
is longitudinal or circular
in shape? Yet, this old man knows better — islands
divide, peninsulas still bind us all
to the creation of the world. And so,
as if obsessed by the sole decent dream,
there he is proving, in the midst of darkness,
the only light that counts — geography
raised to a pulse of ecstasy, a land
becoming the one symbol of God's home.

THE SOLILOQUY OF PHILIP MAZZEI[1]

Adventurer turned dreamer? Let the world
say this of me — that, having crossed the seas
only to learn how man oppresses man,
from the events of one existence I
rescued a dream of justice for mankind.
For it is better that a dream be born
out of adventure than adventure crush
under its rosy tentacles a dream.
Rumbles of revolution in the air . . .
What can they be if not a dream made voice?
Welcome, free music of the rising day,
and spread as fast as sunshine from the snows
of Piedmont to the burnt Sicilian shore,
so that this dreamer finally may rest.
But what is rest? You certainly know not,
old friends of Albemarle, whose action speaks
the liveliness of God since time began —
the very life that bids the spheres preserve
the primal order of the universe.
Why do I suddenly feel young again
as if no storm had gnawed the mountain peak,
and not a single day upon this globe
suffered erosion of inclement night?
Oh, yes! Oh, yes! It only takes the sound
of a familiar name to reconcile
age with eternity, regret with love.
Friends of Columbia! Dear Jefferson!

---

[1]This poem was written for the 250th birthday celebration of Philip Mazzei and takes the form of an imaginary conversation Mazzei is having with his long-time friend Thomas Jefferson.

61

Maybe the sap that nourishes the tree
can hear its own ascent from bough to bough,
and so I, too, my self-renewing force
in all my restlessness from land to land.

How many years ago?. . . Is there a date
for all that we accomplish on this earth
or is our great or small accomplishment
its own eternal calendar of faith?
Forgive me, Sir: I am content to call
man's time my own, and so you must allow
this aging mind to cling to what disproves
its having aged — the dawning of that day
when firmly I set foot on hallowed ground.
Do you remember too? "Virginian"
I called myself in jest, not knowing what
I now know well — that, to renew ourselves,
we have to be our longed-for newness first.
And do you, too, recall how in the breeze
of your fair Monticello I would speak
of men and plants and implements to you
for the rebirth of acres' amplitude?
Oh, but the work of hands implied much more
than simple hoemen's deed: so music too —
woven of twelve soft violins — became
the added magic of your daily care
for the recharging of your human might.

Does music so divert our souls from soil
as to imperil our imported vines?
It does not matter, Sir: we'll drink less wine,
but, as we live for more important goals,
we'll have more water to remind us of
the sober duties of our common fate:
let us be lucid then, lest we be blind.

Sweet friend, dear President! For the old love
that binds two souls into one fervent heart,
am I still free to tell you what I told
the first Assembly of my dreamed-of Land?
If God created all men equal, say:
should inequality on earth endure?
There will be no America so long
as one American is called a slave,
no nation of the free so long as we
ignore the freedom of the weak and poor.
But this and more I told you; now we must
with undiminished faith see that our oath
be not an empty phrase before our God.
There is no blessed future for mankind
if liberty is not man's present gain.

Speaking of Goddess Liberty, my friend,
I have not bent Canova's will as yet.
Tomorrow I shall see him once again,
and, in the midst of all his glorious tasks,
beg him with greater fervor not to fail
the expectation of a friendly shore —
the lasting beauty of our Capitol.
As for the other tokens of your trust,
oh yes, I spoke of my adopted land
once more to France, once more to Poland, Sir.
I can assure you that the ancient sap
has given to both branches its last drops.

Pardon me, friend: a messenger right now
(do tremors of the earth come unannounced?)
has brought me news from Piedmont: victory!
Turin has risen and the people's cry
is echoing along the Apennines —
a call to arms and liberty and love.

I who have fought for other nations, I
have now my own — my Italy at last!
Should I not take possession of my land
while these my eyes can see its radiance?
Have I not earned my future through my past?
'Tis now a question of slow-pacing time
hastened by dauntless spirits. Shall I view,
before I face the Lord, His glory here
on this my earth again? It matters not.
With all these fragrant blossoms on my hill
I do not doubt the certainty of Spring.
So, welcome, Sir, to Italy now free.

THE BALLAD OF FATHER RAVALLI[1]

Father Ravalli comes from heaven every night
back to Ravalli Town to say his midnight Mass,
but no one knows the tale except the very Night
that sees him like a long and lonely shadow pass.

"Father, are you still here? I can't believe my eyes.
You have been dead awhile, and here you linger still
as if there were no room for you in Paradise.
Have you come back to see how old is this old mill?"

"Though I am dead, my son, fear not my living sight,
I asked Almighty God, and this He granted me —
that I could spend on earth one hour every night
in order that I might with all my children be."

"I'm not your son, I'm Night — the time when one should rest
from all the toils and troubles of the laborious day;
but when my silence fell on mountain and on nest,
instead of sleeping, you would either work or pray."

"Forgive me, Sister Night. I bless and thank you still
for the extended time you gave me every eve.
The day was much too short, and there were men to heal,
children to feed and teach, and sinners to forgive."

---

[1]In the state of Montana a county and town are named after Antonio Ravalli, the Ferrarese Jesuit who, together with father Gregorio Mengarini, founded the College of Santa Clara in California. His fame rests on his legendary versatility. Having no formal training in medicine, architecture, the visual arts, and music he nevertheless vaccinated hundreds of Native Americans, built infirmaries and chapels of great usefulness and decourous beauty, was a skillful draftsman and elegant painter, and composed religious hymns. The first mill in Montana was built by Father Ravalli.

"To school of medicine, Father, you never went
and yet you amputated gangrenous legs or arms . . ."

"God was the surgeon — I, but His obeying hand:
and can one ever fail when God alone performs?"

"And tell me: Is it true that music you knew not?
Yet many a hymn I heard, which you yourself composed..."

"'T was but an echo of God's harmony I caught:
I only listened to the singing Heavenly Host."

"Academies of art never admitted you,
and yet you carved and painted as the old masters did . . ."

"I only put on canvas what God had put in view —
beauty of earth and heaven, beauty for every need."

And is it also true that, when a church was built,
nails you refused to drive into the house of God? . . .

"Oh, they reminded me of all my human guilt:
how could I crucify again the Son of God?"

"And tell me . . . never mind . . . I'll ask tomorrow night,
for you are late for Mass and your two angels kneel —
The angels that with you have come in surplice bright
and, when the clock strikes one, will both have done God's will."

Father Ravalli comes from heaven every night
back to Ravalli town to say his midnight Mass,
but no one knows the tale except the very Night
that sees him like a long and lonely shadow pass.

66

GARIBALDI'S CANDLE
(A Soliloquy from Staten Island)

Come, *principale*! To this wonder come!
Look how this candle, dyed white, red, and green,
has suddenly become the only flag
restlessly waiting to be claimed and loved
by the most poor and powerful of lands.
Come, friend Meucci, come, for you and I
must warn the world about this flame we see
before its glory wanes within the night.
Look at its brightness! Have you ever watched
a greater miracle than its new glow,
a more enchanting Spring than its new sheen?
It almost tells we need no other sun
to lead us where we always wished to go —
back to the country God and man call home.
Say, do you see the loftiness I see —
this triple splendor that's one lucent hope
bridging two continents and two despairs?
Oh, answer that you do, or I shall think
that I am dreaming lonesome in the dark
of my own helplessness. See this white glare?
It is the swaddling-bands that, long ago,
wrapped in a crib our open innocence
while, dreaming of our freedom, over us
our mothers sang a lullaby of faith.
And do you see this crimson blaze I see?
It is our very blood turned into flames —
the conflagration of our arid years
longing to reach the first Italian shore

and finally ignite it with its dawn.
And look, Antonio, look! This simple green
is bursting out of centuries of black
to make us know the easy path ahead.
Say, principale, can you see all this?
Yes? I'm not dreaming then. Then, it was God
told me to land where Verrazzano came
so that I might in this your gracious home
encounter one whose dream precedes my own.
Think of the morning when, forever free,
our land will hear your spoken word at last
above the Ocean tamed forever more,
and think, just think of that most solemn day
when in one instant happy light and song
will make our plainland part of God's free world!
Hush! There are envious winds outside that door,
and maybe spies are listening. . . . Let's heed
in silence, then, this candle's last command:
that in the utmost secrecy, right here —
in this small island that no king suspects —
you keep on vanquishing the hostile waves,
and I maintain this sword still bright and sharp
for the impending sunrise of the free.
"Viva l'Italia!" Say it, say it now,
prophetic parrot of the golden beak,
now that we need another friend to trust,
now that — oh, thank you — three of us at least
believe in what our Italy must be.

To Antonin Scalia

Associate Justice, U.S. Supreme Court

Allow my vision not to see in you
Astraea with a pair of scales in hand
or crowned with stars above man's iron age.
Rightly, so long as golden times endured,
she dwelt on earth with lavish gifts of grace,
but sped immortal to immortal light
as soon as men to other men made war.
If I see less in you, then I see more —
a multitude of laborers that land,
lonesome and longing, on a dreamed-of shore
where soon bread turns into affright and woe;
but on they tread from mine to railroad, on
from tunnel to skyscraper, weary, wan,
yet dauntless still through decades of despair;
and when all spit upon them with contempt
and all their hopes are dashed against the sky
and, far from their ignoring native land,
they are ignored and jailed and lashed and lynched
where liberty and justice should be one,
oh, with no weeping (tears have long been shed)
and without talking (words have not been learned)
they stare into the future, not yet theirs,
and see one of them there, one of them there,
where now you sit, Sir, speaking for them all.

THE OLD CHAIR

This chair was once a throne, but of the king
who used to sit in it remains an old,
encrusted pipe — of seventy-six years
of useful life a piece of useless wood
I should discard as such. No diadem
except the imprint of a human head
with some white hair. No scepter save this pipe —
and its smoke rises, a fictitious heaven
enveloping the king once more alive.
I wonder what my Father's dreaming of,
dozing majestic in his favorite chair.
Surely this alien tongue he comprehends
in his own fashion is now taking him
to the far sweeter, more familiar breeze
of his Gargano forest far away.
There, there again, among his childhood friends,
he fails to understand why none of them
can recognize him. He would like to play
with all of them, but one by one, they all
go home and leave him friendless in the street —
in a street named "Fifty-three Years Away."
Or maybe, passing the Canadian border,
he calls the darkest cloud his only friend,
walks miles to reach a paesano's home,
knocks on his door, and asks for work at once.
I wonder what the king is dreaming of.

Now it is I am sitting in this chair,
your only subject, and I only wish,

Father, I'd never told you "Go to sleep,"
now that I know what sleeping really is,
now that I know we only rest our eyes
until the day we open them no more.

FROM SOUTHERN ITALIAN EMIGRANT TO RELUCTANT AMERICAN
Joseph Tusiani's *Gente Mia and Other Poems*

> Quae regio in terris nostri non plena laboris?
> (Vergil, *Aeneid*, I, 450)

Joseph Tusiani's volume *Gente Mia and Other Poems* addresses, with eloquence and dignity, the Southern Italian experience of immigration to the United States. In these few pages (only fourteen of the compositions of *Gente Mia and Other Poems* deal with the immigration experience), Tusiani's muse inspires him to examine the major themes that are associated with immigration: the spiritually and psychologically violent act of division from one's family and native land (which is the first experience of the new emigrant), the dreams of the emigrant/immigrant, the prejudice he/she encounters, the process of Americanization, the question of language, the alienation and the realization that the new world is not the "land of hospitality" (Tusiani 166) he/she believed it was.

"Song of the Bicentennial," an intensely autobiographical poem that opens the collection of *Gente Mia and Other Poems*, examines the above mentioned themes and, after careful reading, leaves the reader with a cynical and somber awareness of what it means to be an immigrant:

> Then who will solve this riddle of my day?
> Two languages, two lands, perhaps two souls . . .
> Am I a man or two strange halves of one?
> Somber, indifferent light,
> setting before me with a sneer of glow,
> because there is no answer to my plight (7)[1]

---

[1] All further quotations from *Gente Mia and Other Poems* will be identified only by the page number.

73

There is no answer to the "riddle" because the immigrant is suspended between two "worlds." As *separation* from the old world becomes complete, the native land acquires mythical characteristics in the mind of the immigrant:

> My long lost land was one that,
> when snows enveloped it,
> did not erase a sun that
> still in my dream was lit
> . . . .
> 'Twas my presepe, full of
> tu scendi dalle stelle-
> the only song and rule of
> intime cose belle. (6)

and, through his *experienced reality*, the immigrant's adopted land has lost those mythical qualities attributed to it by the old timers back in the native village. The new world is presented as unfeeling and cold:

> But now my new found-land is
> the western world, this new,
> mysterious Atlantis
> where men like me and you,
>
> called immigrants, are silent
> when Silent Night is sung
> on this Manhattan Island
> by people old and young,
>
> by all save those, like me
> and you, uprooted friend,
> who think of Italy—
> our lost presepe land. (6)

When reading "Song of the Bicentennial" the reader is immediately struck by three words: *sunder, deracination* and *uprooted.*

> . . . *Sunder* all this — you have
> erosion, desert, and abyss and night,
> Yet I have ceased to be

74

the man I was: the roots wherefrom I sprung
are somewhere else instead. *Deracinated* —
is this the word that somewhat hides the grief
of one *uprooted* and no longer young? (3; emphasis added)

These three powerful words evoke lucid images of the bitter-
ness, violent separation and displacement that for many is the
final *resolution* of the emigration experience. Because of the
dismal social and financial conditions that plagued the *mezzo-
giorno* a whole generation of people was forced to look at emi-
gration as the "lesser of all evils" even though it left the prota-
gonists homeless in the spiritual and material definitions of the
word.[2]

The history of Southern Italians in the twentieth century is
a history of immigration to the North of Italy, to other Europe-
an countries and to North and South America. The uprooting of
individuals and generations of families, caused by powers and
circumstances over which these people had no control, is a so-
cial and historical phenomenon that has been well documented.[3]
It is this reality that leads the poet of *Gente mia* to contemplate
the stars that dot the Southern Italian sky:

The shape — let me be wondering about
the shape of stars that glow,
for something tells me that I too was born
under the sign of one
formed like an ocean liner going far,

---

[2]Tusiani in his article "Deracination and Americanization," refers to two
inquiries on the Italian South commissioned after the Risorgimento, one by
Constantino Nigra, the other by Giustino Fortunato. The inquiry by Nigra
carried out immediately after annexation of the South to the new Italian State
"exposed the inhuman brutality of the wealthy class as well as that of the
clergy in all regions just evacuated by the Bourbons"; the inquiry by
Fortunato suggested "emigration as the lesser of all evils if not the greatest
of all cures. Unnatural and violent though it seemed, emigration meant only
survival just as deracination meant only hope in a new springtime" (152).
[3]Cinematographers have made some of the most powerful statements on the
subject. Films such as *Rocco e i suoi fratelli* (Rocco and His Brothers), *Tre
fratelli* (Three Brothers), and *Pane e cioccolata* (Bread and Chocolate)
examine the emotional trauma, the sacrifice, and the tragedy that stems from
immigration.

crowded with silent men called emigrants —
my ethnic star. (4)

This deliberation on the "ethnic star," a star "formed like
an ocean liner going far," is not a simple romantic notion of ad-
venture to far off uncharted places but the contemplation of the
stark reality of the Southern Italian condition in the late nine-
teenth and the first half of the twentieth centuries, when the
"contadino" had no choice but to become a nomad.

When the emigrant, after a long and wearisome crossing,
arrived at Ellis Island he/she was immediately faced with the first
major obstacle of his new American life — a strange language.
The question of language, or, rather, loss of language, is of pri-
mary importance to our poet when discussing the experience of
emigration. Tusiani introduces this argument in "Song of the
Bicentennial" by a series of questions:

> Do I regret my origins by speaking
> this language I acquired? Do I renounce,
> by talking now in terms of only dreams,
> the sogni of my childhood? What has changed
> that I had thought unchangeable in me? (5)

Tusiani, as far as this author knows, is the only Italian-American
writer who looks at the language question as a spiritual dilemma
more than as a sociological problem (Tusiani 153). The answer
to these questions is that something *has* changed and that every
phrase, every word uttered in English separates him a little bit
more from his roots:

> Now every thought I think, each word I say
> detaches me a little more from all
> I used to love —

For Tusiani when "sogni" becomes dreams, "cielo" becomes
sky, and "mamma" is translated to mother much more tran-
spires than the immigrant's process of Americanization and ac-
culturation. Tusiani, who, besides being a poet, has had a long

76

and illustrious career as a professor of Italian language and literature and as a scholar and translator of Italian classics, knows well the importance of words. Cognizant of the fact that the ideas and culture words communicate goes much deeper than the definition found in the dictionary, the poet knows that "cielo" elicits mythicized visions of the old world and that "sky" will only remind the immigrant of the ghetto in the immense concrete jungle he now calls home, and that when "mamma" is translated to mother a "whole world of feelings and traditions" (Tusiani 154) is lost and the "disintegration of family unity becomes an altogether unpremeditated adverse effect" of immigration.

> Mother, I even wonder if I am
> the child I was, the little child you knew,
> for you did not expect your little son
> to grow apart from all that was your world,
> . . . .
> Yet of a sudden he was taught to say
> 'Mother' for mamma, and for cielo 'sky'.
> That very day, we lost each other. . . . (5)

Loss of the Italian language is for our poet "a betrayal or denial of his original world — indeed his very origin, his very self" (Tusiani 153-54).

* * * * *

Through the poems "The Ballad of the Coliseum" and "The Day After the Feast," the poet takes the reader away from his personal experience with emigration and examines the dreams, achievements, and disappointments of the Italian-American family and the neighborhood: "Little Italy." What historians and sociologists have so well documented in numerous studies, Tusiani conveys to the reader with the sensitivity and insight of the poetic intellect.

In "The Ballad of the Coliseum," which narrates the full history of Italian-American immigration from Southern Italy to New York City, Tusiani tells the story of a simple hard working man who would have gone to his grave unnoticed, as millions before him, were it not for the tragic and news making circumstances of his death:[4]

> That day, he left in all his glory —
> the father of a famous man.
> The Coliseum in the sunshine
> boasted its half completed span —
> a lofty labyrinth of ramparts,
> a mass of steel and wet cement
> that by no blowing wind or thunder
> could broken be or ever bent.
>
> Then, if no blowing wind or thunder
> could shake or shatter it all,
> what sudden wrath of hell or heaven
> struck on a hardly finished wall,
> . . . .
>
> How many dead? How many injured?
> Only one dead — our Angelo. (35)

While recounting the tragic death of Angelo Lombardi, "The Ballad of the Coliseum" brings the reader inside the Italian-American family structure. The family, which is of primary importance to Italian culture, was so essential to the survival of immigrants who were shunned and looked upon as individually and culturally inferior by the mainstream population of the United States. Tusiani makes us cognizant of the forces and unity that bond this fundamental structure.

Insight into Italian-American family life is at the heart of the poem. Forced to leave his family behind in Italy and bearing the tragedy of not being able to be at his mother's side when she died:

---

[4]This poem is based on a true story. Mr. Angelo Lombardi was the only casualty when a wall collapsed during the building of the New York Coliseum. Mr. Lombardi's body could not be found beneath the rubble.

78

> Another day and still another,
>> and then the first and second year . . .
> Time passed and then (O God!) a letter
>> in a black envelope came here.
> "Dear Angelo," it said, "Your mother
>> died of a sudden heart attack.
> She did not suffer, but kept asking
>> until the end, 'Has he come back?'" (31)

Our Angelo uses his savings to purchase "a blessed one-way ticket / for one who soon became his bride" (32) and begins to rebuild the family:

> Many more years went by, and seven
>> boys and a girl, American born,
> calling him Papa! Papa!, made him
>> feel like a king upon a throne.
>
> . . . .
>
> And so our builder every evening,
>> sitting at table with his wife —
> while all enrapt his children listened —
>> counted the blessings of his life. (33-34)

We are also reminded of the important role of *education* in the lives of Italian-American families. Angelo works to make a better life for him and his family. For his children the better life translates into the necessity of a college education:

> . . . .
> The pay is good and — let me tell you —
>> despite my age I feel much stronger,
> well, strong enough to put through college
>> (for time's a-flying) our first son.
> He'll be a lawyer — no, a doctor." (34)

Not losing sight of the *dream* he went "wherever a new building / was being built— uptown, downtown," and for Angelo Lombardi

> Stone and concrete and brick and plaster
>> to him were more than trade and tool:

> they were the miracle from heaven
> that sent his children all to school. (33)

For all of his hard work and sacrifice our protagonist's experience with immigration ends as it had started, by being violently separated from the one thing he held dear — his family. As he was not able to be at his mother's side at the time of her death, his tragic and untimely death denies him the realization of seeing his children fulfill their *American reality.*

"The Day After the Feast," reminiscent of Giacomo Leopardi's "La sera del dì di festa," both in its title and theme,[5] places the reader in the heart of "Little Italy," a geographically well defined "Little Italy" — "the Belmont area of the Bronx in New York with its lady of Mount Carmel on 187th Street and its well-known market on Arthur Avenue" (Tusiani 159). On the day after the feast of Our Lady of Mount Carmel in the Bronx, the poet recalls the festivities of the previous day while life is returning back to normal:

---

[5]Giacomo Leopardi (1798-1837), has remained, for reasons difficult to explain, largely an unknown poet in this country. Born in the town of Recanati, in the Marches region of Italy, Leopardi's life was devoid of the color and drama that is associated with other poets of his era, such as Lord Byron and Ugo Foscolo. His intellectual and psychological makeup were greatly influenced by the forced isolation of his youth. His father, a tyrannical but literate man, demanded that the young Giacomo spend never ending hours at his studies. His education included training in theology, archeology, rhetoric, astronomy, philosophy and languages. By 1817, Leopardi had translated Horace's *Ars Poetica,* parts of the *Aeneid* and of the Odyssey; he had completed several original works, including two tragedies, a *History of Astronomy* and an *Essay on the Popular Errors of the Ancients.* Most important, his extensive contact with antiquity "awakened in him a deep desire to be a poet in his own right."

This formative period also left deep psychological scars on the young Giacomo and ruined his physical health. "The seven years of mad and desperate studies," as Leopardi referred to them, left him a bitter man and his "Canti" and "Operette morali" mirror the profound anguish and loneliness he experienced in his development as a human being and as an artist. For Leopardi the *reality* of adulthood never lives up to the *dreams* that nourish our youth: life is a series of *illusions* destined to be shattered by reality, and happiness is just a fleeting moment between extended periods of resignation and despair.

Last night your children were the chanting throngs
behind your statue and the parish priest,
    and now they once again
are what they were — unknown, hard-working men.

Yes, you are pleased remembering this new
Procession in your honor, with a glare
    of altar boys in red,
a band, balloons slow-floating overhead,

and from the sidewalks people throwing you
signs-of-the cross and kisses and a prayer:
    three hours of paradise
quite visible in all our mortal eyes.

This morning everybody's back to work
as if no holiday had ever been,
    yet everybody's more
resigned to life than ever, ever before. (24)

In describing the parade and feast that took place the previous day, the poet transports the reader into a world and culture that is not American; into a cultural extravaganza that is "part of a centuries old ritual that characterizes the faith of Southern Italians" (Tusiani 159). The religious *festa,* a mixture of pagan lore and Christian belief, is the visual manifestation of the preindustrial culture of Southern Italy. A culture steeped in superstitions, belief in the supernatural and a fatalistic vision of life — *destino.*

For the Italian immigrant in the "Little Italies" of America the *festa* is a means to recapture, if only for a fleeting moment, the illusion of being back in "the old country" where they were understood and "unknowingly try to forget the bitterness of their deracination" (Tusiani 160). As Boelhower states in his book *Looking Through a Glass Darkly: Ethnic Semiosis*, "The feast generically functions as an act of historical synthesis in which each participant feels integrated into the semiotic space of his ethnic culture" (116). This "act of historical synthesis" is, as I have mentioned above, a very short sequence of time and

the immigrant will soon be faced with his/her *American reality*
as the sanitation trucks

> Roaring impassive and iconoclastic,
> . . . devour and crush
> under metallic teeth
> the most impressive *artificial wreath*
>
> along with *cardboard boxes*, empty *plastic
> bottles*, confetti, in a raucous rush
> that nothing spares — not even
> the remnants of man's festive dream of heaven. (25; emphasis
> added)

and New York once again becomes "the city where you hardly
know your street" (25).

The verses just quoted underscore the ephemeral aspect of
the *festa.* The poet gives us images of objects that are not lasting
and are products of an American consumerist throwaway culture:
artificial wreaths, plastic bottles, cardboard boxes. A consumer-
ist culture far removed from the Italian and the Italian immi-
grants' frugal traditions.

Italy, in the mind of the protagonists, is recreated for a day,
but the *festa* is not reality: it is just a vehicle that for a short
time makes the immigrant forget that he lives in a "city where
you hardly know your street."[6]

From the local ethnic level, represented in "The Day After
the Feast," Tusiani shifts his focus to the national level in
"Columbus Day in New York." The Columbus Day celebrations
that take place in large urban centers like Chicago and New York
are a statement to the Americanization of Italian Americans.
Much different than the *festa* described in the "The Day After
the Feast," which celebrates the day of Our Lady of Mount
Carmel, Columbus Day festivities have very little to do with
Italian culture and traditions and, as the poet clearly states,

---

[6]For a clearer understanding of the value of the *festa* in Italian-American
society see Boelhower, *Through a Glass Darkly* (113-17) and Helen Barolini,
Festa: Recipes and Recollections, passim.

Here is the epic of Columbus Day
reduced to an innocuous parade

where mayoral dreamers grin in competition,
endorsed (or almost) by the Governor,
and politicians who are neither-nor
turn on Italian smiles as cars' ignition. (10)

The poet chooses to look beyond the superficiality of the day (the politicians' smiles, the floats, the beauty queens) and sing about the true hero of the day — the unsung laborer with calloused hands who worked and died to make America what it is, and who still is not recognized as "one of her children":

... This is gente mia,
for I can see (is there a lump in my throat?)
dear Christopher Columbus on a float
called for all time to come Santa Maria.

How beautiful he beams! He has the eyes
of my Grandfather, and his calloused hand;
he is the immigrant of every land
unhappy in his happy paradise,

misunderstood in all this understanding (10)

Columbus/Grandfather and the Santa Maria are the powerful symbols that synthesize the history of immigration to the United States:

Look closer! There's grandfather, come this year
to represent Columbus on his float.
A hero and the worthiest of note,
he is the very one no crowd will cheer

tomorrow when the town goes back to work;
but look at him today, today at last,
in all the greatness of his humble past —
the new Columbus conquering New York.

He brings the best credentials to be he —
faith in his glance to win the fighting waves,
dream of free people and despair of slaves
to conquer a new land ultimately.

> So here he is today, today at last
> riding atop his bright Santa Maria,
> the navigator of the gente mia,
> *light of my future, darkness of his past,* (10-11, emphasis added)

The Grandfather figure is the symbol of all the immigrants that have come to this country, who through their sacrifice and suffering *(darkness of his past)* made a better life possible *(light of my future)*. They are for one fleeting day remembered and given their rightful place.

The pomp and gaiety of the Columbus Day festivities cannot hide a bitter truth and the poem ends on a biting note. The recognition is temporary, "he is the one no crowd will cheer / tomorrow when the town goes back to work"; and his destiny is one that robs him of the dignity of his existence:

> the one who came to dig (for dig we must)
> for the high glory of the subway tracks,
> the immigrant who died and yet still lacks
> identity with this American dust. (10-11)

This poem, composed of ten quatrains, accomplishes two things: 1) it reminds America of what Italians have achieved in the new land, from its discovery by Columbus to the humble laborer,[7] and 2) it synthesizes the despair and frustration, of being a *misunderstood immigrant* in a land of immigrants.

Conclusion

Gente Mia and Other Poems reflects on the immigrant's unique dilemma: that of being confronted with two realities, "old world" and "new world," and feeling that he/she does not belong to either. Tusiani, in his search for an answer (or maybe just a

---

[7]Tusiani has published on a number of Italian immigrants in American history: Philip Mazzei, Eusebio Chino, Francis Vigo, and Antonio Ravalli. Poems on Costantino Brumidi, the artist who painted the rotunda of the Capitol building in Washington DC, and Father Samuel Mazzuchelli, frontier priest.

clearer understanding), goes beyond the scientific inquiry of the sociologist and the historian. He delves into the soul and spirituality of the immigrant as he/she quests for a non hyphenated identity and searches for a *patria* in his/her adopted land. The answers he arrives at as a result of his poetic inquiry are not pleasant. *Deracination* (sunder, uprootedness) and *resignation* are what the poet has resolved for himself and his immigrant brothers and sisters. When Tusiani declares "Civicus Americanus Sum: I swore / allegiance to the Flag of Fifty Stars: / Long live America forever more!" he does more so to remind the reader that he, as others before him, has paid the price and belongs in America, more than a nationalistic message.

Through poems like "Columbus Day in New York" and "Song of the Bicentennial," Tusiani shows the reader that the American cultural milieu has integrated the superficial and stereotypical aspects of Italian immigrant culture and has never understood the true character of this populace. The essence of the sacrifice and contribution of the illiterate immigrant with calloused hands has all but been forgotten.

It is up to the poet, who draws his inspiration from the injustice suffered by his people, to assure that their sacrifice will not be forgotten. By so doing the poet also arrives at a definition of his identity and that of his people:

> Now, only now for every suffered wrong
> can I discover who I am at last —
> the multitudinous Italian throng.
>
> I am the present for I am the past
> of those who for their future came to stay,
> humble and innocent and yet outcast. (8)

WORKS CITED

Boelhower, William. "The Immigrant Novel as Genre." *MELUS* 8.1 (1981): 3-14.
____. *Through a Glass Darkly: Ethnic Semiosis*. Oxford: Oxford UP, 1984.

Tusiani, Joseph. *Gente Mia and Other Poems*. Stone Park, IL: Italian Cultural Center, 1978.

____. "The Themes of Deracination and Americanization in *Gente Mia and Other Poems*." *Ethnic Groups* 4.3 (1982): 149-76.

THE WRITER BETWEEN TWO WORLDS
Joseph Tusiani's *Aubiografia di un italo-americano*

> Two languages, two lands, perhaps two souls. . .
> Am I a man or two strange halves of one?
>
> (*Gente Mia* 7)

> Di tutte le lontananze, l'America è la più vera ed esemplare.
>
> (Mario Soldati, *America PrimoAmore* 33)

The theme of the immigrant's flight/escape from a culture of poverty and misery, their *Italian reality*, in search of a better world, the *myth of America*, the immigrant's version of the promised land, permeates the earliest Italian immigrant writings.[1] These Italian-American texts were not considered part of mainstream American literature and much of this writing remained scattered, its literary qualities "naturally overlooked, since the very collective subjects that created their special world view were benignly neglected, buried as most immigrants were in the 'black holes' of the American cosmos" (Boelhower, *Immigrant Autobiography* 18). Fortunately, over the last twenty years the situation has changed. The work of a number of dedicated critics and the publication of a number of studies and anthologies have codified this body of literature, given it a

---

[1]For more in depth studies on Italian immigrant autobiography, see Boelhower, *Immigrant Autobiography in the United States* and Gardaphé's article "My House is Not Your House: Jerre Mangione and Italian American Autobiography," in *Multicultural Autobiography American Lives*, edited by James Robert Payne

Within the context of this essay, when I refer to Italian-American literature, I am limiting myself to the literature produced by Italian immigrants, and not to that body of ethnic literature produced by first-, second-, and third-generation Italian Americans.

definition, and brought it out of the closet, so to speak, and into the public consciousness.

The immigrant author who wants to represent his/her life as an "other," and deal with the conflicts brought about by emigration, spiritual, psychological, and physical, has the daunting task of organizing two diametrically opposed cultural systems, a culture of the present and the future and a culture of memory, into a single working model. Joseph Tusiani's autobiographical trilogy does so very successfully.

The publication of Joseph Tusiani's autobiography in three volumes, *La parola difficile*, *La parola nuova*, and *La parola antica*, connected by the common subtitle, *Autobiografia di un italo-americano,* is in many ways an historical event in the literature of Italian America. With these books, Tusiani marks another milestone in his career as poet, translator, and scholar. In the 958 pages of this trilogy, Tusiani not only narrates his life from the day in 1947 when the "Saturnia" docked at New York City and, at the age of 23, he met his father for the first time, but Tusiani asks us to embark on a voyage, an odyssey that has many different levels of signification. On one level it is the voyage of Tusiani and his family, specifically his mother, who, besides the author, is the other common denominator of the trilogy, from Italy to the United States; from the reality of the Old World, with all its ancestral rituals rooted in a catholic/rural (*cattolico/contadina*) culture, to the reality of the New World, constructed on radically different models. It is a linear voyage in time where the protagonist struggles to create a space for himself in America, in academia and in the world of literature as a poet; simultaneously it is also a circular journey, where Tusiani, maybe unknowingly, returns "spiritually" to the old world — the world of his ancestors. On a different level, Tusiani's recounting of his forty years in the United States takes us on an exemplary voyage through the history of Italian emigration to the United States. Many of the people, famous and not famous, that grace the pages of Tusiani's trilogy, form the essence of Italian emigration/immigration to the United States. For the reader that undertakes this voyage, Tusiani's narrative will evoke many emotions, from the sad to the amusing.

According to Boelhower, the emigrant/immigrant autobiographer has only a choice of "four axiological procedures" from which to proceed:

> The narrator can order his strategy as: 1) a *confirmation* of the codes of the dominant culture (Panunzio); 2) a *variation* of these codes, in which case the dominant culture is respected but some of its untested possibilities are tried (Pascal D'Angelo); 3) a *negation* of the dominant codes (Emmanuel Carnevali); 4) a *substitution* of the dominant culture with a counter-cultural alternative (Jerre Mangione). (*Immigrant Autobiography* 20)

Boelhower uses Constantine Panunzio's *Soul of an Immigrant* as an example of an autobiography that *confirms* the codes of the dominant culture, Pascal D'Angelo's *Son of Italy* as a work where the dominant culture is accepted but a *variation* of the codes is experimented; *The Autobiography of Emmanuel Carnevale* compiled by Kay Boyle as an example of Italian-American literature where the dominant American culture is rejected; and Jerre Mangione's *Mount Allegro* as a work where an Italian-American "neighborhood" is presented as a counter-cultural alternative. Of the four writers, only Jerre Mangione was born in the United States, the others emigrated from Italy.[2] Tusiani's *Autobiografia di un italo-americano* does not fit into the neat categories proposed by Boelhower but incorporates elements from all of Boelhower's proposed "exiological procedures."

From the very first page you realize that Tusiani's autobiography is radically different from the ones mentioned above and from most works of Italian-American literature: *it is written in Italian*. When one looks through the creative works section of

---

[2] Chapter 2 of Boelhower's book analyzes *Panunzio's Soul of An Immigrant*, chapter 3 deals with Pascal D'Angelo's *Son of Italy*, chapter 4 considers Carnevale's view of America, and chapter 5 looks at Mangione's *Mount Allegro*. On Jerre Mangione also see Gardaphé.

the extensive bibliography in Rose Basile Green's ground-breaking volume published in 1974, *The Italian-American Novel: A Document of the Interaction of Two Cultures,* one finds only six books written in Italian.[3] Italian-American writers born in the United States write in English.[4] Interestingly enough, that is the road that Tusiani took once he arrived to the United States; he became an award winning poet in the English Language, and a translator of the Italian classics into English. But, for Tusiani the question of language has always been of primary importance, not as a linguistic exercise, as he stated in his Keynote Address given in 1987 at the 20th Annual Conference of the American

---

[3]These books were written by Bernardino Ciambelli. In 1893 he published *I misteri di Mulberry* and *I drammi dell'emigrazione, seguito ai misteri,* these were followed by *I misteri della polizia il delitto di Water Street* (Frugone e Balletto, 1895), *I misteri di Bleecker Street* (Frugone and Balletto, 1899), *I sotterranei di NY* (Società Libreria Italiana, 1915), and *La trovatella di Mulberry Street: Ovvero la stella dei cinque punti* (Società Libreria Italiana, 1919).

[4]Today there is a whole new group of writers who have recently emigrated to America already culturally formed and who hold prestigious positions in and out of academia who write primarily in Italian, those writers that Paolo Valesio, in his article "The Writer Between Two Worlds: Italian Writing in the United States Today" refers to as "expatriates."

Also, on the phenomenon of Italian-American culture, Valesio writes: "it is worth keeping in mind a motto from the Medieval Scholastics: *Distingue frequenter.* The confusing codes, registers, genres (be they literary or cultural) often leads to reciprocal misunderstandings. In the case of a community such as those 'with a hyphen' (Italo-American, Spanish-American, Afro-American, etc.) the risk is even greater. The danger lies in a growth of pseudo-problems (monstrously mushrooming) that slip into demagoguery. It becomes necessary, therefore, to distinguish between the following:

> 1. Not strictly literary autobiographical and memorial texts, whose collection and systematic analysis is, nonetheless, important for a dialectical understanding of the various components of literary history.

> 2. Novels or short stories written in English by members of the Italo-American community, containing predominance of themes that can be considered characteristic of such a community.

> 3. Works by those that I have called writers between two worlds: the Italian expatriates in the United States who write exclusively or largely in Italian." (273)

Italian Historical Association held in Chicago, but as a sociological and spiritual problem facing the newly arrived immigrant. Tusiani knows, as do most of us who were born in another country, that the emigration odyssey takes many forms. First and foremost, s/he must face, and come to terms with, the actual, physical separation from the country of birth, and from family and friends. This most evident element of the emigration/immigration process is initially the most traumatic. When the immigrant arrives to the new country, the voyage is not finished. S/he will have to undertake other "voyages" in his/her quest to assimilate into mainstream American culture. The most important of these "voyages" is the linguistic/cultural one. S/he must immediately begin the journey from one language, one of the many Italian dialects, to another, American English. Once this process has begun, the emigrant, whose status now is changing to that of immigrant, begins to lose his/her native language and the ideas and cultural values that language transmits; in other words a cultural transformation begins to take place and s/he begins to lose a part of himself/herself. Tusiani first introduced this element so eloquently in "Song of the Bicentennial" through a series of questions:

> Do I regret my origins by speaking
> this language I acquired? Do I renounce,
> by talking now in terms of only dreams,
> the *sogni* of my childhood? What has changed
> that I had thought unchangeable in me? (*Gente Mia* 5)

In *La parola antica*, the third volume of the trilogy, Tusiani returns to the question of bilingualism and discusses it at length:

> Two languages, the reality of eradication (I use this term to indicate total uprootedness) brings on different problems or traumas. First of all that of a new language. Then while learning that foreign language, one runs the risk, for reasons of human vanity, to think of your native language as inferior.
> One does not fall into this trap if the phenomenon of bilingualism is considered not as a conquest but as a forced re-

neging of one's origins and of one's self. Bilingualism becomes synonymous with the disintegration of family unity, for which a mother is not able to understand her own son. From the day when the son says "Mother" instead of "mamma" and "sky" instead of "cielo," between a mother and a son there already is a spiritual separation that the scholar of linguistics cannot catalog. If words are articulated sounds that symbolize and communicate an idea, the term "mamma," different from mother," the newly acquired term, symbolizes and communicates an entire world of sentiments that no foreign expression can comprehend and respect. To abolish it means to renege the existence of a childhood intimately tied to all the episodes, small and large, and to all the emotions, important and not important, connected and inspired by that singular word. Not assimilation or Americanization then, but ambivalence of thought and sentiment, of doubt and certainty, of dream and reality. (*La parola antica* 143-44)[5]

The consequence of this transformation is that the immigrant by expressing himself/herself in the acquired tongue translates not only the language but his/her very soul, and in that process of translation s/he slowly, unrelentingly begins to change. S/he now has the language and the culture of two lands: "America and Italy; in what order though? Should we not say, Italy and America?" (*La parola antica* 143). Tusiani poses these questions because he believes that the immigrant cannot ever be totally assimilated into his/her adopted culture:

To what point can the emigrant assimilate the new language and the new society, and how does he forget and renege himself in the middle of all the new and pressing exigencies of life? Even if the answer lacks scientific validity, the poet tells us that complete assimilation is not possible, that it cannot be possible, and that there can never be complete acceptance, in the spiritual sense, of the traditions of the new land. (*La parola antica* 143)

Tusiani's continuous feeling of "uprootedness" lies primarily within this context of never having fully "spiritually" assimilated into American culture. He perhaps said it best in his "Song

---

[5]Also, see "Song of the Bicentennial" in *Gente Mia and Other Poems.* All translations from Tusiani's *Autobiografia* are mine.

of the Bicentennial," in *Gente mia* (7):

> Then who will solve this riddle of my day?
> *Two languages*, two lands, perhaps two souls . . .
> Am I a man or two strange halves of one?

It is precisely the unsolved riddle, and the feeling of being sus-
pended between two worlds, two cultural systems, that, I believe,
pushes Tusiani to return to Italian, the language of his native
land, for his autobiography.[6]

Another important reason for writing his autobiography in
Italian I gleaned from a conversation that I had with him a while
back. He commented that he did not think it right to translate
the thoughts and words of many of the people that fill the pages
of these three volumes into English. These individuals, although
they lived for decades in the United States, remained primarily
Italian. They never renounced the "old ways" and never under-
stood the "new." These are individuals who did not choose
emigration, but for whom emigration was "voluto da un capric-
cio del destino — voglio dire, dall'inumana legge della povertà"
[due to the fickleness of destiny — I want to say, by the inhu-
man law of poverty] (*La parola antica* 143)

These Italian individuals who lived in the Arthur Avenue
section of the Bronx, "il cuore della piccola Italia" [the heart of
little Italy], are very important to this autobiography. Through
them Tusiani explores the whole phenomenon of Italian emi-
gration to the United States, that Italian emigration that came
to an end after World War II. Their stories, their lives filled
with memories and their attempts to hold on to the "old ways"
enlighten Tusiani about the tragedy of emigration. We meet his

---

[6]Although my statement is technically correct, Italian is the language of Italy
and Tusiani was born in Italy. Tusiani's native language, the language that is
full of cultural significance and remembrances, is, in effect, not Italian but the
dialect that is spoken in San Marco in Lamis. We know that during Tusiani's
youth, living in a small town meant growing up speaking the local dialect as
your first language, standard Italian was a language that was acquired in
school.

uncle Joseph Pisano who entered the United States clandestinely from Canada in search of work. Uncle Joseph who, in his own way continued to love Italy but never returned, and when told of the economic boom of post-war Italy, refused to believe it because it would have meant that all of his sacrifices would have been useless. The Italy he loved was "l'Italia dei suoi ricordi, l'Italia terra di pietre e cardi" [The Italy of his memories, the Italy of stones and cardoons] (*La parola nuova* 132). We meet the Architect Nicola Giusto, who was relegated to menial jobs in the new world because he could not learn English and vented his anger and frustration by having a sign placed over the front door of his house "Qui non si parla il maledetto inglese." Among others we also meet l'artista Onorio Ruotolo, the author Frances Winwar (Francesca Vinciguerra),friend and companion of Tusiani, the poet and labor activist Arturo Giovannitti and Cocò.

Of the individuals that the reader encounters in these three books, the story of Marco Coco, detto Cocò, is the most interesting and, for Tusiani, the most symbolic of Italian immigration. He is introduced in the first book, *La parola difficile*, as "il nume indigete di Belmont, era ormai presso i novant'anni. Ritto robusto energico, eccolo lì, un tantino confuso . . ." [the resident deity of Belmont, was now almost ninety years old. Straight, hardy energetic, there he was, a touch confused . . .]. Cocò emigrated to the United States before World War I and then went back to Italy to fight for his native country in World War I. He came back to the United States where he died at the age of 102 never having renounced his Italian citizenship.

> One hundred and three years old, ninety-two lived as an emigrant. It seemed impossible to me that a boy of ten could not have learned the English language to the point of feeling like an American, like all the other sons and daughters of Italians, who passed through the halls of Ellis Island. Or was our Cocò a special case? Of his native country he only knew the name of the town he was born in, San Marco in Lamis; nonetheless, when someone told him that Italy had gone to war, instead of blessing lady luck for having taken him away from that danger, he was

among the first volunteers to reach his native soil. Was it not his duty to fight for his country, he reasoned. After the war he returned, to the Bronx, the young Marco Coco, more convinced than ever that the greatest joy was that of having served his country: No, he will never become an American citizen, this Marco Coco, because — and it's strange that no one ever understood — you cannot serve two countries. (*La parola antica* 151)

For Tusiani, Marco Coco, whose life spanned the years of mass immigration from Italy, was the symbol of immigration and of all the struggles and injustices that the immigrants had to endure.

The *Autobiografia di un italo-americano* is also the story of two generations of the Tusiani family in America. *La parola difficile,* besides giving the reader a grand tour of Italian-American history, the birth of his American brother, and tracing Tusiani's life from his arrival in New York to the year he won the Greenwood prize for poetry, is about the developing relationship of a man who meets his father for the first time when he arrives in America at the age of twenty-three. The father had emigrated to Italy when, unknown to him, his wife was pregnant with Joseph. Tusiani finally utters the difficult word, "papà," but it takes the almost near-death of his father for him to be able to resolve his conflict.[7] The second volume, *La parola nuova* is the story of Michael, the American son, born one year after his mother arrived in the Unites States, the new son, the one who speaks a different language and who grows up with a world view that is thoroughly different from that of his Italian family. The brother grows up to be President of a major petroleum company. This volume addresses the conflicts, misunderstandings, and difficulties that arise when these two cultures collide. One example, from many in the book, will suffice to illustrate the point. Michael announces to his mother that he is getting married and that the date has been set:

— Maichì — she asked him that same evening when he returned

---

[7]Tusiani first addressed this conflict in the poem "The Difficult Word" in *Gente Mia and Other Poems.*

home — you've already set the wedding date for July, that's OK. Your're still too young to get married, but that's ok. You acted on your own without listening to your parents or brother, and that's also ok. But . . . have you thought about the dowry? What customs do the . . . the Sicilians use in America.

— The . . . what?

— The dowry. I said the dowry

— What's a dowry, Ma?

— You want to get married and you don't know what a dowry is?

— No, I don't know. You tell me!

— Let Giose explain it to you. In Italy one thinks first about the dowry and then about getting married. (*La parola antica* 250)

After it is explained to him what a dowry is, Michael, with his throughly American point of view, explains:

In this land, thanks to God, the poverty that you remember doesn't exist. Here there is work: and that's why what you call a dowry doesn't exist, and that's why a young man named Maichino can marry a young lady named Beatrice without thinking about the hard times I have heard you talk about since the day I was born. You gave me a profession, what else do I need? Beatrice and I will think of everything. (251)

But the dialogue that follows shows that the mother does not understand this line of reasoning. It is a view of the world that is foreign to her way of thinking because she has remained anchored in the culture of her small Italian town:

— But I have to do what we used to do in Italy — interrupted my mother — I will buy your furniture. Beautiful furniture that will be the envy of all our paesani. . . . You have to make an impression like no one has ever done before. One only gets married once . . .

— Mom, in America we have divorce.

— Do not ever say that word again in my house.

— I'm just joking, beautiful mother of mine, I'm just joking.

— These kind of jokes I don't like, Michael.

— But the furniture, Beatrice and I don't want fine furniture; we want modern furniture, that doesn't cost much, because after four or five years we'll want to buy new furniture, and again after that, and . . .

— But, my son, what have these Sicilians put in your head? Furniture has to last you all of your life, and the same for the kitchen . . .

— We're in America, mom, not in San Marco in Lamis. . . . Don't think about these things. We'll choose the furniture, Beatrice and I.

My mother didn't speak anymore that evening. She had never understood America, but now it seemed even more incomprehensible and evil. Good and intelligent as he was, that American son was beginning to break her heart. (251-52)

Mother and son are growing apart, the two cultures, so different from one another, have no middle ground from which to negotiate a common language. They are destined to misunderstanding.

La parola antica, which concludes the trilogy, signals the end of immigration. The word has become ancient because Italian immigration has come to an end, and the cultural conflicts that marked the relationship between Michael and his mother, between Michael's children and their grandmother, will disappear within a generation. The Italian is on the threshold of finally assimilating into American society. For Tusiani "la parola antica" denotes the end of his linear voyage in American society and his definitive "spiritual" return to the land and culture of his birth.

The problem is that forty years of experienced American reality cannot be erased, they have had a profound effect on his life and on his work as a poet, translator, and scholar. In the last episode of the book, Tusiani, on his way back from Italy, dreams that he finds himself alone with his mother in a long corridor bathed by a blinding white light, with many doors on the sides and one door on each end — one which said "Exit," the other, "Entrance." They begin walking toward the door marked "Exit." When they arrive, he notices that it now says "Entrance," and that the sign on the door at the other end of the corridor has changed accordingly to "Exit":

> I arrived under that sign and I read "Entrance." I turned and saw, there where my mother stood, the word "Exit." . . . I retraced my steps, but when I rejoined my mother, high on the wall, in place of "Exit," I again read "Entrance." . . . And forty times, anxiously, pushed by hope and despair, I ran from one end to the other of that enormous corridor.

On the brink of being overtaken by panic, Tusiani notices that the corridor has doors along its sides. On each door is written the name of a person that has had a profound impact on his life: Frances Winwar, Cocò, Onorio Ruotolo, l'architetto Giusto, Giuseppe Antonio Borgese, Louise Townsend Nicholl, Arturo Giovannitti, Martin Luther King, Antonietta Lombardi, an immigrant neighbor, and Father Walsh, a Jesuit mentor. He knocks on all their doors but no one answers. Finally, bathed by the light, he sees the shadow of his father who had died a few years earlier:

> "Father! Father!" I called, while moving toward him, "Mother and I have lost our way, we cannot find the exit."
> "You really are a child." My father answered with a smile, "I know where the exit is, come with me." We began to follow him. (*La parola antica* 309)

The Dream ends abruptly when Tusiani is suddenly awakened by the flight attendant announcing the imminent landing at Kennedy airport. No one can help him find the exit; it is an existential problem to which only he can supply the answer. The book, and the autobiography, ends with this short paragraph:

> Driving towards the Bronx, in the limousine of the Poten Company, I noticed another detail; the windshield wipers, moving from right to left and from left to right, seemed to be saying Entrance-Exit, but I had lost the meaning of those words and for whom they were meant. (*La parola antica* 310)

If the reader does a cursory reading of this paragraph, he or she would probably conclude that Tusiani does not find an answer to his dilemma, and may conclude that he is more confused than ever about his identity. But a closer reading tells us, I would contend, that Tusiani has, after forty years of American life, come to a resolution of his "problem." The resolution is his awareness of being suspended between two worlds, his acceptance of his biculturalism, for which, instead of seeing himself as not belonging to either one or the other world, he can accept himself has being the man of "two languages, two lands, . . . two [socio-cultural] souls," which he had previously questioned in his poetry"

> Then who will solve this riddle of my day?
> Two languages, two lands, perhaps two souls . . .
> Am I a man or two strange halves of one? (*Gente Mia* 7)

After forty years, the riddle has been solved. The questions initially posed in "Song of the Bicentennial" have now become statements.

WORKS CITED

Boelhower, William. *Immigrant Autobiography in the United States*. Verona: Essedue Edizioni, 1982.

The Autobiography of Emmanuele Carnevali. Compiled by Kay Boyle. New York: Horizon, 1976.

D'Angelo, Pascal. *Son of Italy*. New York: McMillan, 1924.

Gardaphé, Fred L. "My House Is Not Your House: Jerre Mangione and Italian-American Autobiography." *Multicultural Autobiography American Lives*. Ed. James Robert Payne. Knoxville: U of Tenessee P, 1993.

Giordano, Paolo. "From Southern Italian Immigrant to Reluctant American: Joseph Tusiani's *Gente Mia and Other Poems*." *From the Margin: Writings in Italian Americana*. Ed. Anthony Julian Tamburri, Paolo A. Giordano, and Fred L. Gardaphé. West Lafayette, IN: Purdue UP, 1991. 316-28.

Green, Rose Basile. *The Italian-American Novel; A Document of the Interaction of Two Cultures*. Cranbury, NJ: Fairleigh Dickinson UP, 1974.

Mangione, Jerre. *Mount Allegro*. New York: Harper & Row, 1989.

Panunzio, Constantine. *Soul of an Immigrant*. New York: McMillan, 1928.

Tusiani, Joseph. *Gente Mia and Other Poems*. Stone Park, IL: Italian Cultural Center, 1978.

____. Keynote Address in *Italian Ethnics: Their Languages, Literatures and Lives*. Proceedings from the 20th Annual Conference of the American Italian Historical Association. Ed. Dominick Candeloro, Fred L. Gardaphé, and Paolo A. Giordano. Staten Island: AIHA, 1990.

____. *La parola difficile: autobiografia di un italo-americano*. Fasano: Schena editore, 1988.

____. *La parola nuova: autobiografia di un italo-americano*. Fasano: Schena editore, 1991.

____. *La parola antica: autobiografia di un italo-americano*. Fasano: Schena editore, 1992.

Valesio, Paolo. "Writer Between Two Worlds: Italian Writing in the United States Today." *Differentia* 3-4 (Spring/Autumn 1989): 259-76.

Joseph Tusiani, Professor Emeritus of Italian and internationally known poet, translator and scholar, was born in San Marco, Lamis (Foggia), in 1924. After receiving his doctorate in English literature from the University of Naples, Tusiani emigrated to the United States in 1947 at the age of 23. In the United States he began his distinguished career as an educator, translator, and poet. From 1948 until 1971, he taught Italian and served as chairman of the Italian Department at the College of Mount Saint Vincent. In 1971 he accepted a position at the Herbert H. Lehman College of the City University of New York, from where he retired in 1983. Professor Tusiani also taught at Hunter College, Fordham Univesity, and New York University.

Among Tusiani's most ambitious translations we have *The Complete Poems of Michelangelo* (1960), Torquato Tasso's *Gerusalemme liberata* (*Jerusalem Delivered*, 1970) and *Il mondo creato* (*Creation of the World*, 1982), Giovanni Boccaccio's *Ninfale fiesolano* (*The Nymphs of Fiesole*, 1971), *Italian Poets of the Renaissance* (1971), *From Marino to Marinetti* (1974). *The Age of Dante* (1974), *Dante's Lyric Poems* (1992), Luigi Pulci's *Morgante* (1998) and *Leopardi's canti* (1999). Into Italian he has translated *Poesie Inglesi*, by Giuseppe Antonio Borgese.

Writing in English, Latin, Italian, and in his native dialect of the Gargano region of Puglia, he has completed several collections of poems. In English we have *Rind and All* (1962), *The Fifth Season* (1963), and *Gente Mia and Other Poems* (1981); in Latin, *Melos Cordis* (1955), *Rosa Rosarum* (1984), *In Exilio Rerum* (1985), *Confinia Lucis et Umbrae* (1992), *Carmina latina* (edited by Emilio Bandiera, 1994); in Italian, *Lo speco celeste* (1956), *Odi Sacre* (1958), and *Il ritorno* (1992); in dialect, *Làcreme e sciure* (1955), *Tìreca tàreca* (1978), *Bronx, America*

(1991), *Annemale parlante* (1993), *Na vota e 'mpise Cola* [Una volta solo s'impicca Cola] (1997), and *Lu deddù* [Il diluvio] (1999).

Joseph Tusiani also published a novel, *Envoy from Heaven*, and a three volume autobiography, *La parola difficile* (1989), *La parola nuova* (1991), and *La parola antica* (1992) with the unifying secondary title *Autobiografia di un italo-americano*.

Joseph Tusiani has received many honors for his writings and for his dedication to education. In 1956, he was the first American to win the Greenwood Prize of the Poetry Society of England. In 1968, he received the Alice Fay di Castagnola Award from the Poetry Society of America and was awarded the Spirit Gold Medal from the Catholic Poetry Society of America. The honor of Cavaliere Ufficiale della Repubblica was bestowed upon him in 1977, the Leonardo Covello Educator award in 1980, and the Leone di San Marco award in 1982. In 1986 the American Association of Teachers of Italian chose Professor Tusiani as the recipient of the first AATI Distinguished Service Award "in recognition of outstanding teaching and/or published research in the fields of Italian language, literature and civiliza-tion." He has also been honored with the Lyons Club Melville Jones Medal for outstanding sevice and the *Enrico Fermi Award* presented by the Enrico Fermi Cultural Center of the Bronx.

Like all writers who are born in one country and received their education in the country of birth, but are culturally and in-tellectually active in another, Tusiani operates in, and from a re-ality that is "bilingual, bicultural [and] biconceptual" (Hicks xxv). He has created literature that explores, is influenced by, and is sensitive to the different cultural and linguistic referents that help mold it. He is a writer writing on and across cultural borders.

With the well known verses from "Song of the Bicentennial" (*Gente Mia* 7), "Two languages, two lands, perhaps two souls. . . / Am I a man or two strange halves of one?" Tusiani perfectly verbalizes the plight of the emigrant/immigrant. In *Gente Mia and Other Poems,* and in the autobiographical trilogy *La parola difficile, La parola nuova* and *La parola antica,* Tusiani addresses, with eloquence and dignity, the experience of immigration to the United States. In these works, Tusiani's muse inspires him to examine the major themes that are associated with immigration: the spiritually and psychologically violent act of division from one's family and native land (which is the first experience of the new emigrant), the dreams of the emigrant/immigrant, the prejudice he/she encounters, the process of Americanization, the question of language, the alienation and the realization that the new world is not the "land of hospitality" he/she believed it was.

As a translator of Italian poetry, Tusiani is clearly the most prolific and one of the most accomplished in the world. His translations encompass all eight centuries of Italian poetry, from short lyrical compositions to some of the most demanding and challenging of the major works, such as the twenty cantos of Torquato Tasso's epic *Jerusalem Delivered,* to the recently published edition of Luigi Pulci's mock-epic *Il Morgante.*

Tusiani is also one of the most prolific Latin poets of our age.

BIBLIOGRAPHY

POETRY

Amedeo di Savoia: Poemetto in isciolti. Pref. Fr. Ciro Soccio. Sant'Angata di Puglia: Tip. Casa del Coure, 1943.

Flora: Liriche. New York: Prompt, 1946.

"Amore e morte" Liriche. San Marco in Lamis: Tip. G. Caputo, 1946.

Petali sull'onda: Poesie. New York: Euclid, 1948.

Peccato e Luce: Liriche. Pref. Cesare Foligno. New York: Venetian, 1949.

Lacreme e sciure. Pref. Tommaso Nardella. Società di Cultura "M. De Bellis" of San Marco in Lamis. Foggia: Stab. Tip. Cappetta, 1955.

Melos Cordis. New York: Venetian, Neo Eboraci, 1955.

Lo speco celeste. Siracusa-Milano: Ed. Ciranna, 1956.

Odi sacre. Pref. Alfredo Galletti. Siracusa-Milano: Ed. Ciranna, 1957.

Alba di Gloria: Dramma Sacro in due tempi per soli, coro e orchestra. Set to music by Michele Bonfitto. Milano: Scuola Eliografica "Figli della Providenza," 1960.

Rind and All: Fifty Poems. New York: Monastine, 1962. Italian edition, *Mallo e Ghermiglio.* Transl. Maria C. Pastore Passaro. Roma: Bulzoni Editore, 1987.

The Fifth Season: Poems. New York: Obolensky, 1964. Italian edition, *La quinta stagione.* Transl. Maria C. Pastore Passaro. Roma: Bulzoni Editore, 1987.

Tìreca Tàreca: Poesie in vernacolo garganico. Ed. A. Motta, T. Nardella, e C. Siani. Illstr. Franco Troiano. San Marco in Lamis: Quaderni del Sud, 1977.

Gente Mia and Other Poems. Stone Park, IL: Italian Cultural Center, 1978. Italian edition, *Gente mia e altre poesie.* Pref. Ennio Bonea, transl. Maria C. Pastore Passaro. San Marco in Lamis: Gruppo Cittadella Est, 1982.

Rosa Rosarum. The American Classical League, 1984.

In Exilio Rerum. Carmina Latina. Ed. Theodorus Sacré. Avignon: Aubanel, 1985.

A Luxury of Light, nineteen poems (seventeen in English, two in Latin ["In Ascensu Domini" e "Rus Hudsonium"]). *Italian Quarterly* (Summer 1989).

Confinia Lucis et Umbrae. Ed. Theodorus Sacré. Leuven: Peeters, 1989.

Bronx America. Poesie in dialetto garganico. Manduria, Puglia: Lacaita Editore, 1991.

Il ritorno: liriche italiane. Pref. Pietro Magno. Fasano di Puglia: Schena Editore, 1992.

Italian Poets in America (special issue of *Gradiva* [1992-1993]). Ed. Luigi Fontanella and Paolo Valesio. 118-18. Answers to the "Questionnaire" 137-38.

Carmina Latina. Raccolta, introduzione e traduzione di Emilio Bandiera. Fasano di Puglia: Schena Editore, 1994.

Annemale Parlante. Poesie in dialetto garganico. San Marco in Lamis: Quaderni del Sud, 1994.

Na vota è 'mpise cola. San Marco in Lamis: Quaderni del Sud, 1997.

Le quatte staggione. San Marco in Lamis: Quaderni del Sud, 1998.

Lu deddù. San Marco in Lamis: Quaderni del Sud, 1999.

PROSE WORKS

Dante in Licenza: Romanzo. Verona: Ed. Nigrizia, 1952.

Dante's "Inferno": As Told for Young People. New York: Obolensky, 1965

Dante's "Purgatorio". As Told for Young People. New York: Obolensky, 1968.

Envoy from Heaven: A Novel. New York: Oblensky, 1965. Translated in Italian by Adriana Valente as *Dal cielo "inviato speciale."* Roma: Ed. Presenza, 1966.

L'infanzia, la giovinezza, l'America, il dialetto, il presente. San Marco in Lamis: Quaderni del Sud, 1999. Interview.

La parola difficile: autobiografia di un italo-americano. Fasano: Schena Editore, 1988.

La parola nuova: autobiografia di un italo-americano. Fasano: Schena Editore, 1991.

La parola antica: autobiografia di un italo-americano. Fasano: Schena Editore, 1992.

TRANSLATIONS

The Complete Poems of Michelangelo. New York: Noonday, 1960.

Lust and Liberty: The Poems of Machiavelli. New York: Obolensky, 1963.

Torquato Tasso. *Jerusalem Delivered.* Rutherford: Farleigh Dickinson UP, 1970.

Giovanni Boccaccio. *Nymphs of Fiesole.* Rutherford: Farleigh Dickenson UP, 1971.

Italian Poets of the Renaissance. New York: Baroque, 1971. Anthology.

The Age of Dante. New York: Baroque, 1974. Anthology.

From Marino to Marinetti. New York: Baroque, 1974. Anthology.

Vittorio Alfieri. *America the Free.* New York: Italian-American Center for Urban Affairs, 1975.

Giovanni Pascoli. "Paolo Uccello." *Forum Italicum* 9 (1975): 428-35.

"Poeti del Settecento tradotti da Tusiani." *Forum Italicum* 10 (1976): 120-35.

Giovanni Pascoli. "Italy." *Italian Americana* 6 (1979).

Torquato Tasso. *The Creation of the World.* With notes by Gaetano Cipolla. Binghamton, NY: Cener for Medieval and Renasissance Studies, 1982.

Ugo Foscolo. "Le Grazie." *Canadian Journal of Italian Studies* 5 (1982).

Giacomo Leopardi. "I canti." *Italian Quarterly* 28 (1987): 109-10.

Dante's Lyric Poems. New York: Legas, 1992.

Giuseppe Antonio Borgese: Poesie Inglesi. Transl. into Italian, introd., annotated, and ed. Antonio Motta. Manduria: Laicata Editore, 1994.

Luigi Pulci. *Il Morgante.* Notes and introd. Edoardo Lébano. Bloomington: Indiana UP, 1998.

Leopardi's Canti. Introd. and notes Pietro Magno. Pref. Franco Foschi. Fasano di Puglia: Schena, 1999.

ESSENTIAL ESSAYS ON TUSIANI'S WORK IN ENGLISH

Cipolla, Gaetano, "Francesca Cabrini: 'Figura Matris' in a Contemporary Novel (J. Tusiani's *Envoy from Heaven*)." *Italian Americana* 1 (1977): 162-74.

Giordano, Paolo A. "From Southern Italian Emigrant to Reluctant American: Joseph Tusiani's *Gente Mia and Other Poems.*" *From the Margin, Writings in Italian Americana.* Ed. Anthony Julian Tamburri, Paolo A. Giordano, and Fred L. Gardaphé. West Lafayette, IN: Purdue UP, 1991.

___. "Images of America and Columbus in Italian American Literature," *Annali d'Italianistica* 1 (1992): 280-96.

___. "The Writer Between Two Worlds: Joseph Tusiani's *Autobiografia di un italo-americano.*" *Differentia* 6 (1994).

___, ed. *Joseph Tusiani Poet Translator Humanist an International Homage.* West Lafayette, IN: Bordighera, 1994.

Petracco Sovran, Lucia. "Problems of Verse Translation from Italian into English: An Interview with Joseph Tusiani." *Italian Americana* 2 (1975): 34-49.

BORDIGHERA PRESS is

BORDIGHERA POETRY PRIZE

The bi-lingual prize for poetry, including book publication, is sponsored by the Sonia Raiziss-Gicp Charitable Foundation. The prize was established to foster the Italian language among Italian-American poets and to offer publication to the best English manuscript by an identifiably Italian-American poet each year.

CROSSINGS: AN INTERSECTION OF CULTURES

A refereed series dedicted to the publicaion of bilingual editions of creative works from Izalian to English. Open to all genres, the editors invite prospective translators to send detailed proposals.

FUORI COLLANA

VIA FOLIOS

A refereed "small-book" series dedicated to critical studies on Italian and Italian/American culture. Works of poetry, fiction, theatre, and translations from the Italian are also published.

ITALIANA

A series devoted to the publishing of conference proceedings.